The "1007 Anonymous" and Papal Sovereignty: Jewish Perceptions of the Papacy and Papal Policy in the High Middle Ages

HEBREW UNION COLLEGE ANNUAL SUPPLEMENTS

NUMBER 4

The "1007 Anonymous" and Papal Sovereignty: Jewish Perceptions of the Papacy and Papal Policy in the High Middle Ages

Kenneth R. Stow

CINCINNATI, 1984

Published with the assistance of
The Henry Englander-Eli Mayer Publication Fund
established in their honor by
Esther Straus Englander and Jessie Straus Mayer

Library of Congress Cataloging in Publication Data

Stow, Kenneth R.
The "1007 anonymous" and papal sovereignty: Jewish perceptions of the Papacy and papal policy in the High Middle Ages

89 p.; 24 cm. (Hebrew Union College annual, supplements.
ISSN 0275-9993; no. 4)
English and Hebrew.
Bibliography: pp. 73–81.
Includes index.
1. Catholic Church—Relations—Judaism. 2. Judaism—Relations—Catholic Church. 3. Papacy—History—To 1309. 4. Jews—Legal status, laws, etc. (Canon law) I. Title. II. Title: "One thousand seven anonymous" and papal sovereignty. III. Title: "One thousand and seven anonymous" and papal sovereignty. IV. Series: Hebrew Union College annual Supplements; no. 4.
BM535.S696 1984 84-25293
296.3'872'0902—dc19 AACR 2 MARC CIP 3/85
ISBN 0-87820-603-5

Typeset in the United States of America by
Eisenbrauns

For Ruth Keren, too

Table of Contents

Foreword

A GOOD DEAL has been said about papal attitudes toward the Jews in the Middle Ages. Almost nothing has been said about Jewish attitudes toward the popes. These Jewish attitudes will be the subject of the following study.

The materials to be studied here, it must be emphasized, constitute only a representative sample. Much information will have to be unearthed and analyzed before a thorough portrait is possible. Nevertheless, I am persuaded that in the long run the validity and representativeness of this sample will be sustained.

This study has taken shape over a number of years. Many friends have done me the service of reading it and offering their criticisms. They include Frank Talmage, David Ruderman, Maurice Kriegel, Esther Cohen, Menahem Kellner and Ivan Marcus. More than anyone else, however, John Boswell labored hard and long. I am also indebted to the members of my graduate seminar at Haifa University, who spent a full semester agonizing with me over the identification of the "1007 Anonymous." But the greatest weight was borne by my wife, Sandra, whose lot it was to listen to my ideas, their revisions, and, yet again, their revisions anew a thousand times over. I cannot thank her enough. Responsibility for what appears in this study, however, is mine alone.

Kenneth R. Stow

The University of Haifa
August 1, 1984

Chapter One
Old and New Views: An Introduction

Popes, Jews and Historians

THERE ARE THREE basic opinions on the subject of papal Jewish relations in the Middle Ages. The first views the popes as the Jews' foremost protectors. The second, in opposition, portrays the popes as seeking assiduously to expel the Jews from Western Europe. The third, taking a midway position, believes the popes were originally sincere about protection, but subsequently allowed outside pressure to tilt them toward repression. All three opinions, however, are unanimous in judging the Jewry policy of both the papacy as an institution and individual popes as well on the basis of the single issue of protection—or, as it is sometimes expressed, the favorable or unfavorable attitude adopted toward the Jews.

This unanimity is the product of many factors, but its primary cause has been a misreading of the proof-texts and stock formulae found in the prefatory clauses (*arenge*) of papal letters. In place of repeating at length the fundamentals of policy in every letter they issued, the popes (through the medium of the Apostolic Chancery) considered it sufficient to justify their immediate actions by supplying brief and perhaps intentionally mnemonic references to such as the notion of "Christian Charity," the idea of "Jewish witness and remnant," or a Psalm commonly understood as forbidding harm to the Jews (often Ps. 59:12). Modern scholars, however, have commonly mistaken these signposts for the totality of the meaning of a specific *arenga*, and, on a broader level, for fundamentals principles and even for papal policy as a whole. As a result, they have interpreted that policy solely in terms of "protection" or "justifications" for a continued Jewish presence in Christian lands, not understanding that protection was an effect alone and not an end unto itself.

The real scope of papal Jewry policy was much broader. Its goal was to define fully the place and role of Jews within the framework of a pure Christian society. That policy, therefore, was complex and elaborate. Reconstructing it requires examining not only papal pronouncements themselves, but also those passages dealing with Jews in the basic works of medieval Christian teaching and doctrine: in particular, the *Summa Theologica* (II, II, 10–12) of Thomas Aquinas, which must be interpreted in the light of Paul (Romans 9–11) and Augustine (*Adversus Iudaeos*), and the scores of canons concerning Jews and Jewish related issues in Gratian's *Decretum*, read alongside the pertinent chapters in the various decretal collections of the thirteenth century.

Together these writings reveal that papal policy rested on a delicate weave of checks and balances designed to insure, on the one hand, that the Jews fulfilled in their daily lives the emblematic and subservient role first ordained for them by Paul in his never transparent discussions in the Epistle to the Romans and, on the other, that Christian society protected the rightful privileges of the Jews it was obligated to harbor in its midst. Papal policy thus aimed at creating an equilibrium between function and presence, making it possible to integrate the Jews into a society structured, at least in theory, according to the tenets of the ideal Christian world order. The maintenance of this equilibrium then became the hallmark of all papal actions involving Jews.[1]

Papal policy, however was not static, rigidly defined and immune to change. Nor was it synonymous with a universal mode of thought; there was no unified opinion on the subject of the Jews. Even Paul contradicted himself, especially in Galatians and Corinthians. In distinction to the soteriologically necessary role he had assigned the Jews in Romans, he implied in Galatians and Corinthians (Gal. 4:21–5:14 and I Cor. 5:5–6:20) that the Jews were primarily a source of social infection whose presence must be shunned at all costs. This idea, which contradicts what would become the articulated policy of the high medieval popes, was brought to full flower in the East by the late fourth century John Chrysostom in his *Eight Orations.* But in a moderated form it also reached Latin Christendom, principally in the works of Agobard of Lyons (ninth century) and Raymond Martini (thirteenth century), whose writings were doubtlessly instrumental in persuading the papacy and other central Church organs to multiply specific restrictions on Jews for what was called the good of society.

The basic flow of papal policy, nevertheless, remained steady. In fact, and as will be shown, the normative policy of the popes exerted a counter pressure tempering the desires of the extremists. Thus, Raymond Martini railed against a demonic Judaism, as Robert Bonfil has argued, but he concluded his *Pugio Fidei* with the reminder that the present moment was not opportune for approaching the Jews. Rather, reaffirming tradition, Martini asserted that it was presently impossible (*minime possumus*) to convert the Jews; their conversion would occur only at the End of Days.[2] In this thought, Martini was joined by his contemporary and one-time Dominican General, Humbert of Romans. Addressing a Chapter of the Order, Humbert wrote in some detail of the Dominican program for teaching Eastern languages instituted to facilitate conversionary activity. His references to Hebrew and missions to the Jews in this address, however, were perfunctory. Furthermore, Humbert, and probably Martini too, subscribed to the idea that contemporary Jews *non sciunt nec possunt contra Christianos.*[3] That is, Jews normally behaved in a peaceful and docile manner (as Christian theology dictated), and, consequently, it was incumbent upon the Church to guarantee the right of the Jews to live in peace and observe their rituals.

Despite the existence of contrasting opinions, therefore, it may be said that the basic principles of papal Jewry policy were implanted in firm soil and resisted erosion. Yet, the identification and description of that policy and its essence: the positing by the popes of an integral role for Jews in Christian society and the attempt to regulate that role by means of an equilibrium involving both restrictions and privileges—have eluded modern scholarship. This is puzzling, for, as will be seen, some medieval Jews did understand papal policy. They even made a point of discussing its political liabilities and advantages.

These Jewish discussions of papal policy will be the subject of the following study. While touching on as many of these discussions as possible, the study will focus primarily on two of them, first, that of Meir ben Simeon of Narbonne in his later thirteenth century *Milḥemet Miṣvah* and, second, that of the anonymous author of the brief, yet intriguing narrative known simply as "The Terrible Event of 1007." It is a text of unexpected richness and must be studied in great depth.

To interpret texts like "The 1007 Anonymous" in the light of current notions of papal Jewry policy, however, would obscure the intentions of their authors. This study must begin, therefore, by examining the formation of papal policy and its basic principles. Parallel developments in the secular domain will also be considered, for the views Jews held of the popes were constructed in no small measure in reaction to what will be shown to be their negative perceptions of royal behavior. On the basis of this examination the reader will be able to proceed armed with the same perspective once enjoyed by medieval Jews.

And yet, it seems unfair to make the reader wait until this examination of policy origins is completed before giving him at least some indication of what the content of Jewish thinking was like. The real point of departure, therefore, will be three brief, but pointed illustrations of Jewish attitudes toward the popes. Hopefully, these illustrations will whet the appetite of the reader giving him the incentive to press on. If for no other reason, they emphasize that Jews truly did comprehend papal policy. Moreover, in their vividness, these illustrations reveal the fundamental reason for undertaking this study, namely, the conviction that the texts now about to be examined express what must have been a central mode of medieval Jewish political thought.

Three Jewish Perspectives

One of the first Jews to recognize the meaning of papal policy was the late twelfth century Ephraim of Bonn. Seeking to explain why the same Jewish communities of the Rhineland that had suffered so devastatingly in the First Crusade had escaped with relatively little damage in the Second, he spoke out unambiguously, saying:

> And God heard our pleas. He sent a responsible priest, a great man and teacher of all priests, one who knew and understood their religion: His name was Bernard of Clairvaux. He too spoke as the Crusaders, (summoning men) to go to the land of the Ishmaelites. But to touch a Jew and take his life, that (he said) would be no less than to assault Jesus himself. . . . And Bernard's words were effective; nor have we heard that he took a bribe.[4]

This is unexpected praise. In 1146 and 1147, the Jews had sought refuge and defended themselves successfully from fortified towers, as Shelomo b. Shimshon, the chronicler of the pillage of 1096–1097, had urged.[5] Nevertheless, without Bernard, his letters and his preaching, Ephraim was now saying, the results might have been catastrophic. It mattered little that Ephraim believed God himself was ultimately responsible for Bernard's actions. Bernard's conscious motivations too had to be taken into account. For, as Ephraim pointed out, Bernard was the leading theologian of the day, "the teacher of all priests," and, as such, he saw himself obligated to uphold the cardinal principle of Christian theology forbidding attacks on Jews under any guise. Similarly, as Ephraim doubtlessly knew, Bernard's protege, pope Eugenius III (1145–1159), had issued a bull—quite possibly at Bernard's urging—prohibiting assaults against Jews and recognizing their right to profess Judaism freely.[6]

Some time before Ephraim, however, Shelomo b. Shimshon[7] had referred to "Satan, the Pope of Rome, the wicked one," who had preached the first Crusade. This same Shelomo had also gone out of his way to note the efforts made by the local bishops in the Rhineland to save the Jews, implying thereby that the pope, who is never mentioned again in the chronicle, was indeed the Devil. He had observed the slaughter yet done nothing to stop it. Nor is there any papal text on the subject of the Rhenish massacres to argue differently, despite the universal disapproval or even condemnation heaped by Christian chroniclers upon the wandering bands that had carried out the rapine.[8] The only major figure who extended himself to protect the Jews, albeit not effectively, says Shelomo, was the Emperor, Henry IV, who dispatched letters of protest from Italy where he had been detained militarily for some years.[9]

Ephraim of Bonn too grants royalty a part in the rescues of the Second Crusade, especially in England and France. But his remarks are brief, and, more than praise the kings, they again emphasize the centrality and efficacy of Bernard. In this one-sided praise of Bernard, moreover, Ephraim was being tendentious. He charged Louis VII alone with cancelling the interest owed by Crusaders to Jews, which was true. Yet, he must have also known that it was Bernard who had implored Louis VII to do precisely this in the concluding paragraph of his pastoral letter decrying attacks.[10] Ephraim's argument, therefore, was purposefully distorted. And, for this reason, it seems fair to view his chronicle, at least in part, in a special light, namely, as a deliberately constructed "position paper" on the correct Jewish response to attacks. The Jews, he was asserting, would do well to look to the Church for help, especially to its highest officials. Whatever else these churchmen felt or did about Jews, their doctrine insisted that in crises they use their full leverage in Jewish defense.

Yet, for all his conviction, Ephraim remained silent about his motives, and he was reserved about revealing why he had deemphasized the value of royal protection and raised the popes and other high churchmen from the rank of Devil to that of agents of rescue. Others, however, were not so reserved, nor were they particularly cautious in estimating how ready the popes were to help. Compared to Ephraim, in fact, they were unabashed optimists, and, consequently, their writings are most informative.

A prime example of this optimism is provided by a Rabbinic Responsum *(Consilium)*, probably of Northern French—although possibly also Italian—origin, composed toward the close of the twelfth century.[11] A local ruler, the Responsum relates, instructs two Jewish creditors, residents of his city, to turn to the pope, the "Head of the Bishops," so they may collect from a debtor. The debtor lived in another city, under episcopal rule; and the bishop of the city had refused to aid the creditors. When approached, the pope orders the bishop to force the debtor to make satisfaction, and the bishop accepts the decision with no demurrer. Most of the debt is then paid.[12]

Two points stand out in this Responsum: First, the title, the "Head of the Bishops," used by the local ruler when he refers to the pope, and, second, the ability to exercise this leadership position with which the pope is credited. They reveal that the author of the Responsum was not only knowledgeable, but also up to date in matters pertaining to the papacy. The papal claim to direct and regular jurisdiction over all bishops had first been made not long before the time of the Responsum itself. The popes had, to be sure, asserted their religious headship of the Church for centuries. And from the time of the Pseudo-Isidorian Decretals in the ninth century, there had been additional claims, originating from both within papal precincts and without, that the popes possessed ecclesiastical juridical primacy. Yet, only from the time of the Gregorian Reform in the late eleventh century had the papacy claimed this primacy unambiguously, and only from that moment did it labor to realize that claim in full. In the famous dispute over the episcopal see at Rheims between Gerbert and Arnulf of Orleans, which took place in the last decade of the tenth century, the latter queried whether Rome could be appealed to and if it had juridical competence in disputes involving extra-Roman episcopal sees. Gerbert, too, the future Silvester II (999–1003), had serious hesitations about such an appeal.[13] The scenario depicted in the Responsum is thus an accurate and detailed reconstruction of an *ideal*, post-Gregorian reality. Beyond that, the secular ruler in this text admits he is powerless to intervene, because he does not want the bishop to "hate me." This phrase suggests a sensitivity to the problem of "ecclesiastical liberties," perhaps the central issue of the Gregorian Reform.

That the reality pictured by the Responsum is an ideal one cannot be overstressed. Searching for a factual model for the Responsum is fruitless. In 1173, Alexander III ordered some churchmen in Poitou to pay an overdue debt to a group of Jews. The cause of the delay, however, was not the unwillingness of a bishop to enforce a loan contract as in the Responsum, but the temporary sequestration, by Henry II, of a prebend whose income was intended to pay off the debt.[14] A mid-thirteenth century letter of Innocent IV to Thibaud of Champagne resembles the Responsum more closely. In response to Jewish complaints, the pope instructed the count to change his policies and not prevent the repayment of legitimate Jewish loans.[15] Yet, here again, the issue was not the question of papal jurisdiction over bishops. It was the manifoldly more delicate problem of direct Church jurisdiction over both lending and the Jews themselves.

The authenticity of the Responsum does not, of course, depend on unearthing specific corroborating evidence. And, for that matter, one line in the text suggests that recourse to the pope in matters related to lending was a regular procedure. But, authentic or not, more important than the events themselves was the manner of their retelling, revealing the preoccupation of the Responsum with theory: The Jews are directed to turn to the pope, *because* he is the "Head of the Bishops." For their part, the Jews take the advice of the ruler and petition the pope, since they *know* he can force the bishop to act. These pointed justifications reveal an author who both knew papal theory and also wished to stress its exploitability. The optimistic tone of the Responsum seems to imply, moreover, that it was sufficient to ask and the pope would order without fail the protection of Jewish rights and property.

This overwhelmingly optimistic view of the pope reflects a mild euphoria going far beyond the positive feelings expressed by Ephraim of Bonn when he spoke of Bernard of Clairvaux. This enthusiasm, nevertheless, seems restrained compared to the attitude of the following text. Toward the end of the thirteenth century, a letter was sent to David Maimuni, the grandson of Maimonides, who was then fighting the attacks levelled against the *Guide for the Perplexed* by Solomon Petit.[16] Shortly after being excommunicated in 1288 for similar attacks, this Solomon visited Rome in search of ecclesiastical support, hoping to renew the precedent set in 1233 when Church authorities in Montpellier had ordered a burning of Maimonidean writings. Contrary to Solomon's expectations and requests, however, the pope is said to have issued a *breve* praising the *Guide*—"whose wisdom was boundless (at least when it did not contradict Christian truth)." Those who dissented from this opinion and prevented the study of Maimonides, the *breve* continued, would be fined the sum of one-hundred pounds.

Notwithstanding the regular use of Maimonides' writings by scholastic philosophers,[17] accepting the legitimacy of this *breve* involves straining the imagination. If for no other reason, its author could have only been Nicholas IV (1288–1292), whose reissue of the bull, *Turbato corde*, implicitly licensed the Inquisition to reexamine Jewish texts and determine anew if they insulted Christianity. The euphoric belief in the efficacy and reliability of the pope, it thus appears, had progressed to the point of fantasizing.

But such fantasies were not representative. On the contrary, by the thirteenth century certain Jews had acquired a good deal of perspective, and some of them were producing distinctly sober analyses of papal-Jewish relations.

The source of these analyses was the ability of a few insightful Jews to see the continuities linking the principles underlying papal theory as a whole to the principles governing papal Jewry policy. In particular, they had identified a series of concepts that had coalesced sometime in the twelfth century and from that time on had served as the basis of a formalized policy. They had also perceived that unlike the kings, who had shown themselves to be increasingly arbitrary and difficult in their dealings with Jews, the popes were proving themselves consistent with respect to the privileges, as well as the limitations, their policy established. Papal consistency and predictability were, in fact, the major revelations of the Jewish thinkers, and it was because of these qualities that they unfailingly advocated the acquisition of papal support, as was seen in each of the three texts just reviewed.

Yet, can this notion of the predictability of papal Jewry policy be substantiated? It certainly varies with the commonly accepted opinion depicting that policy primarily in terms of alternations between periods of relative calm and even privilege and periods of draconian restriction. Restrictions, moreover, have been called the norm, especially from the thirteenth century. And to support this assertion, scholars have pointed to the edicts of the Fourth Lateran Council of 1215, the assault on post-biblical literature and contemporary Jewish practices in the 1240s, and the all-encompassing and ofttimes papally supported offensive of the Dominicans, which began in the mid-thirteenth century and included censorship, occasional missionary Hebraism, and the attempted manipulation of the papal inquisition.[18] Nevertheless, these outbursts of repressive energy did not sidetrack medieval Jewish thinkers as they have many moderns. Always keeping in mind the complex foundations of papal policy toward the Jews and the necessary connection between that policy and policy for the Church as a whole, medieval Jews thought, rather, in terms of modulations within a basic continuity. Why they thought this way and why they were convinced they were correct in doing so will now be investigated. As indicated above, however, this investigation will begin by examining the formation of that papal policy on which this thought rested.

Chapter Two
The Growth of Papal Policy

Fundamental Principles of Papal and Royal Policies

The foundations of a papal Jewry policy were laid in the late sixth century by Gregory the Great. Borrowing his phraseology and ideas from the Theodosian Code of 438, he stipulated that Jews who agree to live by the limitations of the law (and in particular the law of the Church) would be guaranteed their peaceful existence and the free practice of Judaism within Christian lands.[19] By the twelfth century, this stipulation had come to form the heart of the bull, *Sicut Iudaeis*, or, as it is also called, the *Constitutio pro Iudaeis*. The fundamental clauses of this bull reiterate the principle that law-abiding Jews have been taken under papal protection and thus are entitled to the benefits of Christian *Caritas*: They are not to be molested, attacked, falsely accused, baptised, or have their property seized without due legal process. Reissued a score of times between the twelfth and sixteenth centuries, at both papal initiative and Jewish request, this bull became the primary text of papal policy. In the thirteenth century, *Sicut Iudaeis* was absorbed into the *Decretals* of Gregory IX, thereby achieving canonical status and permanent validity.[20]

Between the sixth and twelfth centuries, however, no pope renewed Gregory the Great's teachings on the Jews. In their place, came the threatening language of Stephen III (772), warning Christians to stay away from Jews, lest the sons of light be endangered by the sons of darkness,[21] and the theories of Agobard of Lyons and his school, grudgingly conceding the Jews a place in Christian society.[22] In Agobard's view, the Jews were the *impedimentum* blocking the way to perfection of the *Populus dei Christianus* and symbolizing all that was evil. Continuing the tradition established during the patristic period, moreover, in the early medieval period, heresy was considered, as well as named, judaizing.[23] There was thus little reason for Jews to trust the popes and none whatsoever for anyone to argue that the popes should be approached for help of any kind. There certainly existed no articulated program for dealing with the Jews.

In contrast, early medieval secular rulers regularly granted Jews writs known as *tuitio* charters establishing a series of direct and mutual obligations, including that of special protection, between sovereign and subject.[24] In addition, these rulers, and kings in particular, had proved themselves unreceptive to the ideas of radical bishops, like Agobard. Louis the Pious may have accepted the episcopal premise that Jews must be regulated by Church canons. But, just as he rejected claims to subordinate royal to episcopal interests in general, so he also rejected the specific extremes proposed by Agobard and his successors in the name of canons for the Jews.[25] Doubtlessly as cognizant of these developments as they were of those within the Church, Jews—from the ninth century through at least the time of Shelomo b. Shimshon—must have concluded that it was politic to trust the king.

This situation would not last long. No hard evidence exists permitting the confident reconstruction of Jewish legal history between the ninth and eleventh centuries, but it is clear that by the time of the First Crusade significant changes had occurred in the legal status of the Jews and in the picture just drawn. The *tuitio* charters, once granted as a means of additional protection for those who *already were* permanent residents and fully integrated into the fabric of society had now become the *sole written legal basis* for a Jewish presence in a given territory.[26] While, that is, various kinds of written law with a territorial basis were developing throughout Western Europe, the Jews had begun a slide into legal and constitutional isolation. This slide would reach bottom in the thirteenth century with the growth of Chamber Serfdom and other similar statuses prescribing the total dependence of the Jews on the kings and dukes whose *quasi-Catallum* they had become.[27] Even when, for example, it was understood that on an ongoing basis, Jewish complaints would be aired in local courts under normal rules of legal procedure, it was no less understood that this arrangement existed only as long as it suited royal or ducal pleasure.

The Jews thus became vulnerable to the manipulations of their rulers, and especially of those rulers who hoped thereby to extend the scope of their prerogatives. These manipulations, however, did not always succeed. Fearful that through them the kings would gain unfair and perhaps illegal benefits, the barons sometimes reacted sharply. The best known of these reactions resulted in the clauses in the *Magna Carta* preventing the king from indirectly controlling the transfer of estates and inheritances by exploiting his powers over Jewish lenders and lending.

Additional royal concessions in England in matters concerning Jews were hence the equivalent of a *Confirmatio Cartarum*, the reconfirmation of the *Magna Carta* forced upon the later thirteenth century English kings more than once by their rebellious barons.[28] This English example is the most vivid; numerous other examples of the Jews being treated as an object in dealings between kings and barons could also be brought from France and Germany. But the point should be clear: As such an object, caught between the king and his barons, or between any two groups in friction, the Jew quickly came to be portrayed as fulfilling exclusively negative functions.

This negative portrayal of the Jews did not proceed from any one group or class. The Jew was viewed on all levels of society as the disrupter of laws and feudal obligations, the agent of economic exploitation and moral destruction, and the dissident, opposed to universally shared beliefs and opinions. High medieval lay society, in other words, created an image of the Jew not dissimilar to that held by certain members of the clergy in the Carolingian age. The wave of exhilarated lay piety that peaked in the twelfth and thirteenth centuries and to which kings were no less susceptible than the barons, or any other of their subjects, then made the image all pervasive.[29] It would take only the occasional service of Jews in such tasks as royal executioner to turn the metaphor of Jewish destructiveness into actual fact.[30]

The stewards and members of what was consciously on the way to becoming the nascent political, mystical and religious body, known otherwise as the incipient modern state, thus joined together in the belief that they must shield themselves and the *patria*[31] from the danger to social harmony and overall unity posed and symbolized by the presence within their midst of the Jewish stumbling block. Urged on by clerical purists, secular society voted unanimously to rid itself of the Jews.[32] There was, after all, no constitutional or legal roadblock in the way. The royal "owner" had only to assent. And he, sooner or later, resolved the conflict between the demands of piety and the "commonweal," as opposed to any potential benefit to his prerogative—let alone any inherent Jewish right, by deciding in favor of the former. This decision was invariably accompanied by renewed baronial and, sometimes, clerical support, or the diminution of baronial opposition.[33]

Jews certainly took note of all of this. Some, like many Sephardim after 1492, were never able to relinquish what has been termed the myth of the royal alliance.[34] Others, reflecting on their civil status, realized they must not place their hopes on the crown. But they also had to find an alternative. Medieval society would not allow anyone, and certainly not the Jews, to function in a vacuum.

In the long run the alternative to the crown was found in the Church. In distinction from the kings, the Church was ultimately bound by its theology, in particular, the teachings of Paul (in Romans) and Augustine and the dormant precedents of Gregory the Great.[35] Certain churchmen, of course, had rejected these teachings, like Chrysostom, who had called for the elimination of the Jews.[36] But Chrysostom's writings were not directly known in Medieval Europe, and even his followers in the spirit, like Agobard, had recognized that the law and teachings of the Church made room for and insisted upon a Jewish presence in Christian society until the End of Days.[37] Whence, at some point the Church would have no alternative to drawing the implications of its theology and establishing a clear cut and formal policy regarding the Jews, with whom it was destined and obligated to live.

Such a policy emerged during the eleventh century. And it was no accident. For it was at this moment that the Church began to gain control of itself and of its administrative structures,[38] and, so too, it was then that the Church at last became capable of identifying its real enemies and not feeling threatened by fantasies. Armed with these capabilities, the Church could now define with precision the role of its various members and also of those *qui foris sunt*. But in this light, it must be clear that the basic difficulty the Church faced in defining the relationship between Jews and Christians was not, as is often thought, one of finding a balance between the two competing tendencies of toleration in opposition to the will to repress or even eliminate the Jews from Christian society. It was, rather, in arriving at a formula justifying the retention of Jews *within* Christian society while simultaneously exploiting the Jewish presence to advance Christian teachings and interests. These included, of course, matters related to papal theory. Just as the popes claimed primacy in Christian society in all matters concerned with spirituality, so they would appoint themselves the guardians in all spiritual affairs concerning the Jews—whether they be in the realm of Jewish Christian relations or, even internally, in the realm of what the popes claimed was proper Jewish religious behavior.[39] More than anything else, it was this assertion of guardianship and its broader implications that Jews would come to ponder most.

Sicut Iudaeis *and the Maturing of Papal Jewry Policy*

An articulated papal Jewry policy was inaugurated by Alexander II in 1063. In three letters, the most well-known of which entered Gratian's

Decretum as *Dispar nimirum est*, the pope first recalled the normative Pauline-Augustinian theology of Jewish rejection and punishment and then praised the efforts of the Viscount and Archbishop of Narbonne, as well as the body of Spanish bishops. In response to an earlier papal request, these churchmen had restrained the warriors under their command and prevented a Jewish slaughter during recent military operations in Spain. Going beyond simple recognition of service, however, and with the apparent intention of turning a precedent into a rule, the letters also specified that the protection of Jews was proper, for the matter of the Jews was entirely different from that of the Saracens: The latter actively engaged in war against Christians; the former were everywhere ready to be subservient.[40]

By subservient, Alexander II meant inferior and willing to accept domination. Like Gregory the Great before him, Alexander was repeating the threat of the Theodosian Code demanding that Jews refrain from contempt for the Christian law lest they lose all their legal privileges.[41] But Alexander was also implying that as the Church waged a Just War against the Saracens, Christianity's active enemies, so would it declare forfeit the otherwise unassailable right of the Jews to reside in Christian lands—and wage war against them, too—if, like the Saracens, they began to oppose Christian rule.

Alexander II then made a further point. He stressed the need of upholding the teachings of Paul and Gregory the Great emphasizing the rightful claim of the Jews to Christian Charity and stipulating their necessary role in Christian soteriology. Hence, the pope was refining earlier ideas, insisting that the protection of the Jews involved a careful balance of *both* Jewish and Christian obligations with which neither Jews nor Christians could take liberties. Christian protection of the Jews was thus to hinge, as if contractually, on the implementation of the precepts of Christian theology, on the one hand, and the acquiescence of the Jews to Christian sovereignty, on the other. This insistence on mutuality—so concisely expressed by Alexander II, although masked at times in the letters of his successors by a rhetoric of frustration often bordering on exasperation and sometimes rage—was to become the permanent basis of papal dealings with the Jews.

But a Jewry policy could not rest on *Dispar nimirum* alone. A more lucid, detailed, and mature expression of that policy was needed, if only to focus the scores of canons dealing with Jews and the particulars of Jewry policy that had been and would continue to be formed over time. This expression came sixty years after *Dispar nimirum* in the crisp wording of the bull, *Sicut Iudaeis*. The greater sophistication of *Sicut*

Iudaeis should not, however, obscure the common purpose and underlying conceptions uniting it with *Dispar nimirum*. The continuity from *Dispar nimirum* to *Sicut Iudaeis*, as the following discussion will show, is truly self-evident.

What is not self-evident is that both texts were products of the involuted political climate of late eleventh and early twelfth century Rome. An investigation of the specific circumstances leading to their promulgation, therefore, should be most useful. For the fact that two such carefully constructed texts were issued despite the unstable political climate suggests that an understanding of these circumstances will provide the answers to a number of questions: First, whether a well-wrought papal Jewry policy indeed emerged in the late eleventh and early twelfth centuries; second, whether this policy rested squarely on fundamental principles of Christian theology; and, third, whether a consensus had grown within contemporary Church circles that this policy was just and its right to endure unassailable.

In approximately 1041, one Baruch of Rome converted to Christianity, married a Frangipani, and founded the house of Pierleoni, which numbered among its direct descendents the Antipope, Anacletus II (1131–1139), and included among its relatives popes Gregory VI and Gregory VII.[42] By Jewish law and canon law, too, the Pierleoni were Christians. But for the popular mind and for contemporary political opponents, they were something else. Thus, in the 1060s, Benzo of Alba spoke condescendingly of Leo, the son of Baruch (Benedictus), saying: *Iudaeus erat, Iudaice loquebatur* (He was a Jew and talked like one too);[43] and bishops Arnulf and Manfred wrote of Peter II (Anacletus), *Iam nec Iudaeus quidem, sed Iudaeo deterior* (Now not a Jew in fact, but worse than one). Even St. Bernard, who was one of the prime movers in the party of Innocent II in opposition to Anacletus, could not refrain from questioning Anacletus' suitability for the papal office, because of his supposedly impure ancestry.[44]

This whole episode did not pass the Jews unnoticed, as attested to by the legends of Elḥanan, the Jewish pope.[45] More pertinent, this episode may have effected the Pierleoni too. Seeing the unwillingness of those around them to forget their Jewish ancestry, first after twenty and then after ninety years (and probably many more times in between), the Pierleoni may have become responsive to a Jewish call for distress—notwithstanding their undisputed zeal for the Church, Gregorian style reform and anti-Imperialism[46]—and unlike many later converts who were to turn into the Jews' principal antagonists.

The Pierleoni may also have had no choice in the event of such a call. The Roman territory controlled by the family embraced the traditional zone of Jewish residence near the Teatro di Marcello. Following normal medieval civic patterns of organization, in which clans, clientage, and areas of residence were often interlocked, the Jews of Rome must certainly have been Pierleoni dependents.[47] Unrelated to any sense of a common lot evoking feelings of a shared concern, therefore, the Jews had every reason to expect protection from their patrons. And this was true even if, as Jews—and second class citizens in Rome—their clientage too was of a second class nature.

Protection of Jews was, furthermore, a topic capable of producing a positive response in papal circles at this time. The papally sponsored Spanish military campaign of the 1060s[48] had stimulated the growth of two ideas: First, on a specific level, the concept of a special papal status of feudal sovereign in Spain,[49] and, second, on a broad plane, the theory of the Just War.[50] The distinction drawn between Saracens and Jews in Alexander II's letters of 1063, defining the Saracens as an active enemy against whom an attack was legitimate, aided the Just War theory. The further implication that by not harming the Jews, the Christian warriors were respecting papal wishes and effectively accepting the pope as their legitimate military commander reinforced the claim to Spanish sovereignty.

The crucial element bringing together the matters of blood, clientage, Just War and pretensions to sovereignty was the degree of papal dependency on the Pierleoni. In 1060 and again in 1120, the occupants of the papal chair, Alexander II and, then, Calixtus II, owed their position to Pierleoni support in election disputes that had dragged on vociferously and often violently for years.[51] Aside from any other considerations, this last matter would have made a Pierleoni request on behalf of the Jews hard for any pope to refuse. An approach by the Jews of Rome to their Pierleoni patrons, whether in 1063, at the behest of their Spanish counterparts,[52] or in 1120, for their own sake, could have led directly to the issuance by Alexander II of the letter containing what would become the future canon, *Dispar nimirum*, and, then, to the promulgation of *Sicut Iudaeis* by Calixtus II.

Perspective, however, must not be lost. The intervention of the Pierleoni was only a catalyst. The texts of *Dispar nimirum* and *Sicut Iudaeis* were not the tendentious products of bribery or favoritism; their contents, as seen, reflect accurately the traditions of Christian law and theology. *Sicut Iudaeis* was also not innovative in its format. With its grant of privileges predicated on the Jews having been taken under papal protection or wardship (*tuitio*), the bull was a patent reworking of those *tuitio* charters of Louis the Pious that had been incorporated into Carolingian formulary books, and its immediate paradigm was the *tuitio* charters the papacy itself had frequently dispensed to monasteries far from Rome, in places like Northern France.[53]

At the same time, the renewal of Gregory the Great's doctrine of protection in the letters of Alexander II and Calixtus II did not mean the popes had abandoned the traditional Church demand for Jewish limitation and restriction. *Dispar nimirum* leaves no doubt about this, and the point may be seen again by noting that Hildebrand (the future Gregory VII) undoubtedly had a say in the drafting of Alexander II's letters of protection. Yet, this did not prevent Hildebrand as pope from issuing a letter in 1081 prohibiting Spanish Jews from possessing public office.[54] The balance between privilege and restriction in the dealings of the popes with the Jews is most evident, however, in *Sicut Iudaeis*. The entire thrust of the bull is to guarantee the rights of those who have asked for protection. But it is also understood that these petitioners are fully prepared to accept the dominion of the Church and to submit themselves unquestioningly to its laws and controls.

This compatibility of *Dispar nimirum* and *Sicut Iudaeis* with all aspects of Christian tradition was crucial. Because of it, the policies they announced did not disappear. The two texts, it cannot be overemphasized, had not simply made a flimsy statement of protection supported by little more than a biblical text warning against the killing of Jews (like Psalm 59:12) and possessing only transient value. Rather, they had proposed a clear cut framework for the existence of Jews within Christian society. This framework was going to prove itself firm, consistent, and unyielding to the vagaries of individual papal whim.

This point of consistency and continuity has, nevertheless, been the subject of doubt, and it has been particularly obscured by the matter of papal efforts made on behalf of the Jews during the First Crusade. Familiar only with the maledictions of Shelomo b. Shimshon, most historians have claimed there were no such efforts. They have also claimed *Sicut Iudaeis* was issued in 1120 as a belated response to earlier papal failings, intended to forewarn Christians everywhere against future attacks on the Jews.[55] A close look at *Sicut Iudaeis*, however, reveals that originally, it could have applied only locally. For one thing, its prominent *tuitio* clause, indicating a Jewish request and a papal response, would have appeared nowhere except in a text between a ruler and his immediate subjects. Not even the popes would have so audaciously used a *tuitio* clause with reference to the subjects of another ruler, whoever he may have been. And this was true, even if by the twelfth century such clauses had lost much of their earlier importance and were no longer the true regulators of legal status between governor and governed. Indeed, the only extra-territorial recipients of papal charters containing *tuitio* formulae in the early twelfth century were certain monasteries which, by common consent, enjoyed a special relationship with the papacy. All other recipients were residents of territories under direct papal rule. In pointed contrast, in the thirteenth century, when the papacy began to claim a measure of direct rule over all infidels, including Jews—a matter on which more will be said further on—it also began employing the *Sicut Iudaeis* bull, with its *tuitio* clause intact, universally.

The local applicability of *Sicut Iudaeis* may additionally be inferred from those sections of the bull threatening desecrators of Jewish cemeteries. Yet, most illustrative is the clause insisting that Jews be tried and punished according to strictly legal procedures, what would be called a "due process" clause in present-day terms. From the point of view of the Jews themselves, this clause was probably the most important element in *Sicut Iudaeis*, guaranteeing the legal foundations and stability of their existence. There was to be no arbitrariness and all privileges were to be honored in full. No twelfth-century pope would have considered conferring such fundamental privileges upon Jews living beyond his immediate control. At the most, when speaking of all Jews, a pope of this period would have gone no farther than repeating the declaration of Alexander II against indiscriminate attacks.

This last point may explain the actions of Urban II in 1096. By the time of the First Crusade, the three letters of Alexander II, together with an additional text of Gregory the Great on the subject of protection (that does not contain the *Sicut Iudaeis* clause), had been absorbed into the *Decretum*, the canonical collection prepared in 1095 by the French ecclesiastic, Ivo of Chartres.[56] So placed, the letters would exercise considerable influence. Their directives would be accepted by the French bishops responsible for the official crusading army. And with the possible exception of one outburst in Rouen, these bishops did succeed in preventing attacks on the Jews of France. But these bishops were also allied to their countryman, Urban II, so that even in the absence of hard evidence, it seems fair to judge his actions and intentions on the basis of theirs. Urban, that is, must also have accepted the principles of

Alexander II as set forth in *Dispar nimirum*.[57] Moreover, if the evidence provided by an anonymous chronicle composed no earlier than two hundred years after the time of the First Crusade is at all reliable, there is no need for speculation, and Urban's motives may be positively determined. For, says the chronicle: "In the same year (1096), R. Yosi b. Levi went (from Ashkenaz) to Rome (the pope—who, in this case could have only been Urban II) and returned with a bull (*ḥotam*) annulling the forced conversion."[58]

All of this stands in stark contrast to the situation in the Rhineland. There, the recognized head of the Church was not Urban II, but the Imperial designee, Wibert of Ravenna (Clement III); his position vis-à-vis the Jews was the precise opposite of that just attributed to Urban II. Despite the opposition of Henry IV, Wibert denounced the return to Judaism of those Jews who had been forcibly converted during the attacks.[59] When Shelomo b. Shimshon spoke of the pope, therefore, he was certainly referring to Wibert, whom he had confounded with Urban II.[60] And, in this light, it is not surprising that he also confounded Wibert with the Devil himself.

The Jews of Rome were better informed. They had understood the position of Alexander II, Ivo of Chartres and Urban II quite well, and they had no question about the constancy of papal protection. Accordingly, in 1120—although Rome was still in turmoil at the end of a three year struggle over the possession of the papal crown—the Jews of the city turned to the pope and petitioned his help. The result was the bull, *Sicut Iudaeis*.

Non-Jews too had come to appreciate the newly announced papal teachings. Christian chroniclers of the First Crusade widely condemned the slaughter of Rhenish Jewry—although after the fact and with a question mark about the obscure ways of divine justice. And with the preaching of the Second Crusade in 1146, responsible Churchmen sought to prevent the slaughters from reoccurring. The most notable of these churchmen was Bernard of Clairvaux. Despite his belief that the Jews were *personae non gratae* possessed of a bovine mentality, he still felt obliged to denounce the sermons of his pupil, the monk Rudolph, whose crusading zeal and call to the body of Christians in Rhineland to reenact the events of 1096 had made a mockery of the aims and principles of his teacher.[61] It was for specifically this denunciation that Bernard earned the praise of Ephraim of Bonn. Bernard, however, was not alone in grasping the Jewish predicament. With or without his intervention, Bernard's other pupil, Eugenius III, reissued *Sicut Iudaeis* in 1147.

Whether Eugenius was responding to a limited request of Roman Jewry or a wider one cannot be stated confidently.[62] Yet, what is important here is the decision to respond to such a request by reissuing specifically *Sicut Iudaeis*. This decision marks the beginning of a consensus. The protection of the Jews and the limits of that protection, it would soon be widely held, could be defined only within the framework of a much broader definition stipulating the basic conditions Jews and Christians must accept if a Jewish presence in Christendom was to continue. *Sicut Iudaeis* provided just such a definition, and, accordingly, it was this bull and no other that was reissued. Nevertheless, this is somewhat paradoxical. For Bernard and Eugenius III, the men who were now actively protecting the Jews and constructing a framework enabling them to remain within Christian society, were among the most active members of the party that had opposed the Pierleoni, the Jews' erstwhile patrons, in the great struggle between Anacletus II and Innocent II in the 1130s.[63]

Patronage, it thus seems, was no longer necessary if protection was to be had, nor was party affiliation. On the need to affirm the protection of the Jews and their privileges, the leadership of the Church, soon to be followed by the majority of the hierarchy, was now in agreement. At the same time, as the text of *Sicut Iudaeis* further shows, these Church leaders were also in agreement on another point. Jewish protection and privileges were not to be granted unconditionally. In any articulated papal Jewry policy, protection and privilege had to be balanced by Jewish subservience. Consequently, in his summons to crusading arms with its warning against attacking Jews, Bernard recalled the principles of *Dispar nimirum*. And despite Ephraim of Bonn's attempt at concealing the facts in his chronicle, the truth is that Bernard did call for a limitation on Jewish lending activities. Likewise, over one hundred years later, in his outline of goals for the Second Council of Lyons in 1274, in which he discounted the possibility of a Jewish danger to Christian society, the former Dominican General, Humbert of Romans, made a point of specifying that the Jews were a "subjected people" (*subiectos*) and were to be treated as such.[64]

What churchmen like Bernard and Eugenius, as well as those to come after them, like Humbert of Romans, were most concerned about establishing, therefore, was not whether a Jewish presence in Christendom was simply to be tolerated. What they had to define was the correct place—the assets and liabilities—of the Jews in the Christian world order. For they understood well that in this order, the Jews, symbolizing at once the absence of belief and the hope for the ultimate universal salvation, possessed an integral role.

As for the complete definition of that role, it may be seen in its full maturity in the hundred or so canons of the *Decretum* concerning the Jews and the equal number of laws found in the various Decretal collections of the thirteenth century and afterward. A synthesis of these canons and laws is also available in the comprehensive and retrospective *De Iudaeis et Aliis Infidelibus* of Marquardus de Susannis, composed in 1558; its late date should not obscure the intrinsically medieval viewpoint of its expositions of pure law. Alternately, a lengthy theological discursus appears in the discussion of Judaism as the absence of faith in the *Summa Theologica* (II,II,10–12) of Thomas Aquinas. Summary definitions, too, were produced. Perhaps the pithiest was the maxim of the doctors of Roman law, like Baldus de Ubaldis, who asserted that Jews (living peacefully) were *fideles* of the Roman Church Militant.[65]

Nowhere, however, is the definition of the Jewish role in Christian society more apparent and nowhere is it more succinctly or elegantly set forth than in the text of *Sicut Iudaeis*. If, therefore, *Sicut Iudaeis* was originally a product of the turbulent political realities of its day, its importance—like that of its predecessor and companion piece, *Dispar nimirum*—far transcended these immediate circumstances. Notwithstanding the severe shocks it was to receive from events like the condemnation of the Talmud in the 1240s and the initiation, shortly after, of inquisitorial proceedings against alleged Jewish fautors of heresy, both the bull and its teachings were going to enjoy the support of all of the popes and the bulk of the ecclesiastical hierarchy; and its doctrines would remain in force, fundamentally unmodified, until 1569.[66] Certain perspicacious Jews understood these facts perfectly.

Chapter Three
Jewish Perceptions of Papal Jewry Policy

Basic Trends

How quickly Jews came to appreciate the true importance of *Sicut Iudaeis* cannot be precisely established. Ephraim of Bonn knew the bull was valuable, but only a few years earlier, Shelomo b. Shimshon (writing around the middle of the twelfth century) seems not to have appreciated the bull at all. His opinions were likely influenced by the inability of the Churchmen in the Rhineland to afford protection in 1096, irrespective of their intentions, while Wibert of Ravenna's decision about the fate of the forcibly baptized must have removed any remaining doubts he may have had. The long tradition of legislation in local ecclesiastical councils insisting on Jewish social segregation, which was sometimes issued in mordently vilifying terms, would not have encouraged him to reverse his thinking either.[67] For Shelomo b. Shimshon, and doubtlessly the bulk of his contemporaries, therefore, the Church was only a source of danger. They would not remold their attitudes without some significant reason.

This reason was provided by the unprecedented forcefulness of Bernard of Clairvaux in demanding protection of the Jews during the Second Crusade. Only in the aftermath of his example did Jews begin assessing the complexities and usefulness of Church doctrines. A complete remolding of Jewish attitudes did not occur, however, until the end of the twelfth century. For it was only then that Jews became fully aware of the expanded role the popes were playing in Christian society and the degree to which the popes had established their hegemony in the realm of what they had termed "spiritualities" and "ecclesiastical liberties." From this time forward, however, Jewish discussions of the Church, the popes, and papal Jewry policy display a constantly growing awareness of not only papal realities, but of the minutiae and most recent developments in papal theory as well.

Jewish opinions on the papacy are various and diverse. They range from simplistic naiveté to intimate awareness. As an aggregate, the popes appear as the supreme rulers of Christendom, or as its joint rulers along with the emperors. They are the source of ultimate legal authority in matters pertaining to Christianity, and for the Jews, at least, they symbolize the Christian religion and its meaning, at times with eschatological overtones. The popes, most importantly, are the single firm source of Jewish protection and the last place for appeal in the face of royal capriciousness.

These opinions reflect, of course, political theory. They do not represent any form of Jewish allegiance to the papacy or its programs. It was politic to build up the papal image, and had anyone cared to seek their opinion and support, many Jews would have readily enlisted in the extreme papalist camp. What mattered for the Jews, therefore, was not whether the popes claimed certain powers; as far as the Jews were concerned, the papacy, like all of Christianity, was a chimera. What counted, rather, was knowledge, first of the intricacies of papal theory and then of its applicability: Did Christian society accept papal political theory, and was it willing to permit the implementation of that theory even if this led to Jewish advantage.

Despite this concern, most Jewish opinions on the papacy were either expressed as fragmentary interjections or confined to the elucidation of single facets of papal activity. The twelfth century Responsum discussed in Chapter One, for example, was interested solely in the question of the papal headship of the Church and the episcopacy. This point returns in a twelfth or thirteenth century interpolation in the *Sefer Yossipon*, which, like the Responsum, calls the pope the "Head of the Bishops."[68] Eventually, texts like the excoriation of the apostate, Paul Christian, written by Jacob b. Elie,[69] elevated the pope to the "Head of the Nations." This title soon went into common use. It appears, for instance, in a 1354 petition to the King of Aragon[70] and in the sixteenth century chronicle of Eliyahu Capsali. Capsali used the term repetitively, and provocatively, applying it to the Emperor, as well as to the pope.[71] In this usage, Capsali had been preceded by the mid-thirteenth century Meir b. Simeon, and the latter had gone even further by calling the Emperor the "Head of the Nations" in pointed contrast to the King of France.[72]

Jews also created parables about papal powers and functions. In his Commentary on Talmudic aggadot (legends), Isaac b. Yedaiah assigned the pope a role in the apocalyptic activities surrounding the advent of the messiah.[73] And, similarly, Nachmanides described the pope as

Pharaoh, vaguely linking him to the angel, Michael, who is to set the Jews free at the time of the Fourth Kingdom.[74] This figure suggests knowledge of Joachimist-like teachings of some sort, especially those of Peter John Olivi, or what in the present context may be best compared to the teachings of an alternative pope, the Angel Pope, and an alternative papacy.[75] Simeon b. Zemah Duran went beyond this by having the pope announce the arrival of Antichrist.[76] In fact, Duran probably saw in his contemporary, Benedict XIII, whose policies were so exceptional,[77] Antichrist himself.

Of particular interest to Jews was the ability of the pope to stand above divine law, at least the Gospel law that Christians accepted as divine. First disparaging the intentional modesty of the title, *servus servorum dei*,[78] the thirteenth century *Sefer Yosef Ha-Meqane* then expressed its doubts about the claimed apostolic power of binding and loosing.[79] These doubts reoccurred in the *Sefer Nisaḥon Yashan*[80] of the same period. But they were especially prominent in the writing of Profiat Duran,[81] who was followed by Hasdai Crescas[82] and then Yosef Albo[83] during the Conciliar epoch, when such matters as the right of the pope to dispense from the Gospels and his prerogative of being "judged by none" were called into question.[84] Crescas and Duran also cast aspersions on the legitimacy of the Petrine succession of the popes from Jesus.[85]

Given this fairly accurate knowledge of the papacy, and of papal monarchism in particular, there is every reason for assuming that some kind of rounded theoretical construction underlies the references to papal aid and protection found in such diverse texts as the *Disputation of Rabbi Yeḥiel of Paris*,[86] its contemporary, the *Letter of Jacob b. Elie*,[87] the thirteenth century polemic, *ᶜEdut Adonai Neᶜemana*,[88] and the early sixteenth century *Shebet Yehudah* of Shelomo ibn Verga.[89] Indeed, the author of the *Nisaḥon Yashan* even knew that the Talmud was condemned at Paris in the 1240s for the specific crime of being a *Nova Lex*,[90] a corruption, and not the unfalsified Mosaic Law, whose observance alone the Church permitted in witness to Christian truth.

From the mid-thirteenth century, moreover, any Jewish theory about papal Jewry policy could be verified by citing numerous examples from practice. The popes had denounced pogroms and blood libels, sanctioned the collection by Jews of moderate rates of interest, responded to petitions to reexamine the Talmud to determine whether parts of it were not blasphemous and, hence, permissible, and placed limits on inflammatory sermons and inquisitional excesses.[91] The popes, of course, had also allowed the original confiscation and burning of the Talmud or, alternately, its censorship, the establishment of forced preaching, if with reservations, and the extension of inquisitorial powers to Jews who had purportedly aided converts returning to Judaism.[92] Nevertheless, the popes had stipulated that these activities be carried on without arbitrariness and, especially, "without infringing the privileges conceded the Jews by the Apostolic See."[93] Consequently, if the popes failed on occasion to gain the cooperation of lay leaders, as well as certain members of the Church hierarchy, in enforcing these stipulations, this fact must be interpreted carefully[94] and not equated with the lack of a well defined Jewry policy or a commitment to preserve the Jews' legitimate rights and privileges. Why else, it must be asked, did the Jews constantly petition the popes for redress[95] and for intervention on their behalf with secular rulers? As noted above, however, most Jewish authors refrained from expressing their overall views on the papacy and limited themselves to but disappointingly brief remarks on all of the above subjects.

The Milḥemet Miṣvah

In contrast to these diffuse images of the papacy, the mid-thirteenth century *Milḥemet Miṣvah* of the Narbonese scholar, Meir b. Simeon, contains the germ of a coherent picture.[96] This picture also has a well defined context even if it does represent some wishful thinking—as Meir b. Simeon himself readily admitted in the section of his work entitled: "The Letter I would have Liked to Send to King Louis."[97] Besides this letter, Meir recreated a number of purported exchanges on the subject of lending at interest he had with the Archbishops of Narbonne, Guillaume de la Brou and Gui Fucois, the future Clement IV.[98] Here Meir laid out his basic theme. On the one hand, he attacked the policies of St. Louis, which, from the 1250s, prohibited recouping even the principal of loans. On the other, he cited both conciliar decrees and the pronouncements of papal legates specifically allowing the collection of a moderate rate of interest. The Archbishops should accept these precedents, Meir argued, while rejecting outright the policies of the king with their blatant perversion of justice. In practice, as Meir admitted, the Archbishops took a cautious midway position, sanctioning the collection of the principal, but not the interest on loans already made.[99]

The contrast between papal protection and royal depredations is brought out most strongly in the "Letter to the King." The pope, Meir pointed out, conducts himself with the Jews on the basis of fixed legal standards: Unlike the king, who arbitrarily annuls oaths and covenants, the pope, "The Vicar of Christ," upholds them.[100] Meir may have reached this conclusion by observing actual practice, but he may have also been influenced by taking note of theoretical principles too. A 1233 letter of Gregory IX, for example, insisted that legitimate loan contracts with their oaths of observance not be voided.[101] Meir's adamant declaration that if the king did not observe the divine law concerning oaths, the pope certainly did is, thus, not to be wondered at; nor should there be any surprise that Meir claimed he instructed Archbishop de la Brou not to go on acting as though the King knew more of canon law and theology than did the pope.[102]

Meir's efforts to applaud the pope and disparage the king are seen again in his lengthy discussions of forced preaching and the burning of the Talmud. For all the detail, the papal role in these events is simply glossed over,[103] although Meir was well informed about what had taken place. He knew the pope was culpable to some degree; if the pope had not initiated the events, he had acquiesced to them and given his consent. However, what concerned Meir was his constant desire to pit royal arbitrariness against papal compliance with the rules. And, in particular, he wished to establish the pope as the paragon for those who would insure the right of the Jews to profess Judaism without hindrance. In an obvious allusion to the clause of *Sicut Iudaeis* guaranteeing the Jews the observance of their "good customs," Meir wrote forcefully: "The pope does not forbid us to lend at interest, for that would be to forbid us our religion, which permits us to lend to non-Jews."[104] Meir did not wish this fact obscured, even at the price of ignoring such delicate issues as the involvement of the pope in the burning of the Talmud.

With all this, Meir was a realist, especially when it came to the ecclesiastical hierarchy. The hierarchy was, after all, not immune from royal influence. It had vacillated on the issue of lending at interest, and not merely out of fidelity to the literal wording of the canons. And it had assented to certain arbitrary actions the king had taken on the grounds that the Jews were his direct dependents. Meir thus reasoned that one must deal most carefully with the clergy and with the members of the hierarchy in particular. They had their limits, and the Jews must learn them.[105] For this same reason, Meir also counselled against exclusive reliance on the pope. Not only was his control over the bishops and prelates incomplete, but certain Christians openly rejected his leadership, especially the heretics who fought him in bloody battles. Accordingly, Meir did not hesitate going beyond the pope and pointing to the example of the Emperor. In his Code—which Meir cited St. Louis for violating—the taking of reasonable interest was indeed sanctioned.[106]

Meir's reliance on the pope, therefore, was tempered. And he noted tellingly that if the pope was the Head of the Nations, the same had also been said of the Emperor. Nor, he went on, was there a lack of kings ready to challenge the imperial monopoly on world rule.[107] But this was not just political fact, it was also high theory: Did the pope possess one sword, or two, and if two, were kings and Emperors obligated to accede to papal commands in all spheres and at all times? Was there, moveover, a unified Empire and a single Emperor, or were kings in their kingdoms not the equals of the Emperor and, hence, independent of him? These, of course, were pivotal questions, and they formed the subject of tenacious debates on the part of Christian theorists, both lay and clerical, in Meir's own day.[108] Yet, did not one of the claims in the arsenal of the legist protagonists of these debates declare that a measure of the Emperor's all embracing rule was that: *Etiam Iudaei sub eo sunt*?[109] Meir b. Simeon, one imagines, must have known this claim verbatim.

A mature and highly sophisticated approach to the world of the thirteenth century and its leaders thus emerges from the *Milḥemet Miṣvah*. The papacy is a force that can work to Jewish advantage, yet it is neither sufficiently powerful nor secure to guarantee its constant reliability. Nor is any individual pope a friend. The popes grant and protect what the canons permit, but no more. If advantage is to be had from them, they must be approached knowingly and with a full awareness of their limits.

The Limits of Papal Action

The "1007 Anonymous" and the Time of Its Writing

What were the limits of papal power? Meir b. Simeon, who was perhaps more concerned with denigrating the king than with lauding the pope failed to offer a precise definition. Indeed, he scattered his thoughts about the pope throughout the *Milḥemet Miṣvah* rather than gathering them into one cohesive unit. It was left for another author, whose subject is specifically the pope and the Jews, to spell out the limits of papal protection.[110] The narrative he wrote in order to do so, however, is far from transparent. It is not even possible to know his name. So well concealed is his identity, in fact, that his narrative has misled more than one modern reader, particularly with respect to the time of its composition. In order to appreciate this narrative, therefore, it will first be necessary to digress and determine when it was written. The great value of its contents fully justifies this digression.

The narrative tells of an attack and forced conversion purportedly occurring in the year 1007 and brought about by the refusal of the Jews of France to make of themselves "one people" with the others through apostasy. Initiated by King Robert the Pious, at the urging of his lay counsellors alone, and following an inquisition into the nature of Jewish "knowledge" (probably referring to the Talmud and other similar works), the attack was carried out by various elements of the populace, some of whom are called simply "enemies," but with Richard, Duke of Normandy, specifically mentioned. Appearing first as a principal antagonist, Richard eventually responds to a miracle, temporarily halts the persecution, and accedes to the request of one Jacob b. Yekutiel, a Jew of Rouen, that he be allowed to go to Rome. Upon his arrival there, Jacob petitions the pope—who remains unnamed and who, Jacob claims, has jurisdiction in such matters—to decide on the legitimacy of the persecution. The pope does this and declares the persecution illegal. Then, after reiterating the clauses of *Sicut Iudaeis* and winning the assent of his bishops, the pope dispatches a legate to demand the immediate cessation of all violence. Jacob's mission completed, he returns home to "Lotharingia," a hero, and with a papal blessing to send word to Rome if ever again the Jews are threatened. Shortly after his return, however, Jacob departs again in order to settle in Flanders, where, but a brief time later, his soul flies heavenward in holiness and purity.

This story has long been considered legitimate—if for no other reason, its Christian characters (who are all named except for the pope) correspond to specific early eleventh century figures, and the time of its writing has been judged contemporary to the events it describes.[111] Comparisons, too, have been drawn, showing what appear to be clear parallels between 1007 (as I shall hereafter identify the narrative) and three eleventh century Christian texts, the Quedlinberg Annals and the chronicles of Raoul Glaber and Ademar of Chabannes. All three of these texts speak of attacks and persecutions of the Jews. Long ago, however, Isidore Levi rejected this mode of proof out of hand. Quite correctly, he saw the comparisons do not hold up.[112]

Only the Quedlinberg Annals tell the story of a royally initiated persecution, that of Henry II in Germany.[113] But unlike the 1007 the subject is a local expulsion, and, judging from comparative Jewish sources, it lasted for barely thirty days.[114] Raoul Glaber, with great detail, links widespread attacks on the Jews (which he says took place about forty years before the time of his chronicle, ca. 1045–1049) with a Jewish plot leading to the destruction of the Jerusalem Church of the Holy Sepulchre by Muslims in 1009.[115] Yet, no hint to this supposed plot is found in 1007; it lists the refusal of the Jews to convert as the single cause of the persecution. More pertinent, the sole instigators of 1007's persecution were Robert the Pious and his lay counsellors. Glaber credits "the common will of all Christians." He also speaks of episcopal support,[116] while in 1007, it is the bishops who advise the pope to bring the violence to a halt. In any case, in the account of the Holy Sepulchre plot in the third text, the chronicle of Ademar of Chabannes (which preceded that of Glaber by twenty years, ca. 1020–1029), there is no reference to an attack on the Jews. Glaber's story thus appears doubtful, and there is good reason for suspecting that Glaber was writing about what he would have wished to befall the Jews and what he would have wanted the bishops to do, but not at all about real events.[117]

Returning to Ademar, his chronicle does contain a persecution story, but its locus is Rome, not northern France. In the year 1020, he reports, Benedict VIII ordered a number of Roman Jews burned at the stake for allegedly desecrating a holy image and thereby causing a severe outbreak of plague.[118] Such brutality, however, would hardly have elicited the praise found in 1007 for the contemporary pope. For following the chronology in 1007, that pope may well have been Benedict VIII himself.[119]

Another, indirect comparison has been drawn between 1007 and Robert the Pious' well-documented offensive against the heretics of Orleans in 1022.[120] The two stories have fascinating parallels: royal initiative, an active role played by the Duke of Normandy, as well as by the Queen, and, most important, the errors of the heretics themselves. Christ, they taught, was not born of a virgin, did not suffer for men, was not truly laid in the tomb, and did not rise from the dead. The sacraments of baptism and the Eucharist, as well as the invocation of saints, were nothing but sheer folly.

For obvious reasons these errors could have easily been labelled "judaizing." Indeed, early medieval churchmen had used this term freely, employing it with reference to numerous deviations from orthodoxy, irrespective of any actual link between Jews, Judaism and the heterodoxy in question.[121] The term eventually became so common that Edward I once instructed his judges to proceed against Christian usurers for judaizing, that is, lending at interest.[122] In this light, it might be fair to presume that the events of 1007 and 1022 were somehow interrelated and that Robert the Pious attacked the Jews in the year 1007 for judaizing and proselytizing among Christian heretics. But if so, then why did both Ademar and Glaber, who were otherwise anxious to report Jewish plots and crimes, not even hint in this direction? And why did they not see the events at Orleans as a direct continuation of the royal offensive against judaizing that had commenced in 1007? In fact, not only did they fail to link the two episodes, but, like the other chroniclers who deal principally or tangentially with the life of Robert the Pious,[123] neither Ademar nor Glaber mentioned the events of 1007 at all.

A comparison of the 1007 narrative with potentially relevant eleventh century Christian chronicles, therefore—whether directly, indirectly, or by inference—does not substantiate that a persecution took place. Such a comparison, rather, leads to the conclusion that there was *no* persecution, and, in particular, one launched by King Robert the Pious. Hence, the 1007 narrative appears to be a fiction.

A link, nevertheless, may exist between the 1007 narrative and the events of 1022. As might be expected in the light of what was just said, however, that link is a purely literary one. The specific date of 1007, for one thing, may derive from an error in a manuscript of Glaber's chronicle, which places the Orleans episode in 1017. This date could easily have become 1007 when written in Hebrew characters, although, regrettably, the unique extant Hebrew manuscript of 1007 does not corroborate this point.[124] As for the overall literary connection, the author of 1007—who, as will be seen, was both well-versed in Christian literature and wished to make his point through a parable—may have been attracted to the Orleans story precisely because of the judaizing content of the heresy. With Jews substituted for the heretics and with the pope introduced into the plot, this story now provided him with the vehicle he otherwise lacked, allowing him to express his own will most vividly. And that was to describe the delicate status of the original judaizers, the Jews themselves, in their encounter with the complex array of medieval governmental forces claiming sovereignty over them in one respect or another.

A revised Orleans story also served another purpose. Despite its lack of historicity, 1007's author did want his readers to believe his narrative was authentic. Yet, such a convincing fiction could best be constructed on the basis of a reliable eleventh century historical model, and preferably a Jewish one too. The only candidate for this model, however, the Hebrew dirge describing the forced conversion of the son of Rabbi Gerson ben Judah, the Light of the Exile, was too well known and too commonly accepted to be used.[125] Still—against the background of this account, as well as the reality of the constant stream of conversions to Christianity, forced or otherwise, that did occur in the eleventh century, culminating in the First Crusade disasters of 1096—the author of 1007 could hope to remold an appropriate story of non-Jewish origin and convince a Jewish audience of its truth (especially in the much later period when 1007 was actually written). He found such a story in the Orleans episode of 1022.

In hoping to succeed with his fiction, 1007's author may have also been exploiting another eleventh century reality: the appearance of popular chiliastic ferment early in the century (to be distinguished from the sixteenth century legend predicting the onset of the apocalypse for precisely the year 1000). Twelfth and thirteenth century Jews were aware that similar ferment had been partly responsible for the tragedies of the First Crusade, and it is thus probable that they would have accepted as true the story of a royal persecution which, like the Crusade, also took place at a time of well-known popular excitement, that is, in the year 1007.

A modern audience, however, should react differently to a story of this sort. Present day research has shown that leading eleventh century churchmen, nobles, and even the Emperor, Otto III, acted vigorously to suppress contemporary chiliastic ferment.[126] But these actions certainly did not include unprecedented persecutions, and chief among them a royal attempt forcibly to convert the Jews of France. Persecutions of this sort would have only aroused popular furies and fantasies, not calmed them. The events surrounding the chiliastic ferment of the early eleventh century, therefore, serve only to reinforce the impression that the 1007 story is a pure and deliberate fiction.

To make this point, however, it is not necessary to rely exclusively on indirect evidence. The 1007 narrative exposes itself directly. Bits and pieces of the story—on the whole, the very morsels presenting its theory of papal Jewish relations—do not correspond to eleventh century realities, but reflect those of a much later time.

First, the descriptions of martyrdom by suicide in the narrative bear a striking resemblance to similar descriptions in the mid-twelfth century crusade chronicle of Shelomo b. Shimshon, including the common use of identical phraseology: to wit, "they stretched forth their necks to the sword," and, more revealing, *Ḥasidei ᶜElyon* (the Righteous of the Heavens), referring to the martyrs themselves.[127]

Second, had 1007 been written in the eleventh century, its hero, Jacob b. Yekutiel of Rouen, could not have returned from Rome, as the text states, to his "family in Lotharingia." Until 1106, Lotharingia (Lower Lorraine) was a distinct geographical and political unit located southeast of Brabant. In the eleventh century, therefore, Jacob b.

Yekutiel, "from the city of Rouen" (in Normandy), could not have *returned* to Lotharingia.

At a later time, however, this was not an impossibility. In 1106, Lotharingia merged with Louvain and eventually (1190) became part of the Duchy of Brabant. Upper Lorraine, too, bordering Champagne on the northeast, and named Lorraine after the eleventh century—although it was never a distinct political unit like Lower Lorraine—slowly dissolved and, in 1218, was absorbed by the County of Champagne.[128] This geographical fluidity is particularly reflected in medieval Hebrew texts. An early twelfth century letter from the Jewish community of Paris to that of Rome speaks imprecisely of Lothair as one of the four main regions of France: Tsarfat, Lothair, Burgundy, and Normandy.[129] Similarly, in texts of Jewish legislation produced by councils meeting in Champagne in the late twelfth century, the term, Lothair, refers to territories stretching from Normandy to the edge of the Rhineland.[130] Both political realities and the frequent disregard of the Jewish sources for geographic precision, therefore, solve the problem of Jacob b. Yekutiel's return to "Lotharingia." His journey could have ended almost anywhere in northern France, assuming, of course, that the time—at least the literary time—of his return was no earlier than the later twelfth century, and quite possibly even later.

Jacob b. Yekutiel's eventual settlement in Flanders raises a further geographical difficulty. The careful researches of Jean Stengers have concluded that although Jews had settled in Brabant by the eleventh century, they did not arrive in Flanders until the thirteenth. This conclusion has been summarily dismissed by Salo Baron, but the basis for his dismissal is solely the 1007 Anonymous, which Stengers, for his part, quite rightly finds untrustworthy.[131] Apart from that, to assume that people as reputedly important as Jacob b. Yekutiel and his family settled in Flanders in the eleventh century, as Baron claims, while no further evidence of Jewish life in that province is to be had for another two hundred years, places too great a demand on the imagination.

Jacob b. Yekutiel's settlement in Flanders would have been apposite, however, in a tendentious context, if, for instance, the author of 1007 wanted to make all traces of his hero disappear: The absence of these traces, and the absence of any record of Jacob b. Yekutiel's descendents, in particular, the author may have believed, might discourage readers from questioning the authenticity of the narrative and the correctness of its all important theories. Nevertheless, arguing this point requires assuming that 1007 was written no earlier than the thirteenth century. For then Flanders did have a Jewish community, and readers might not have wondered about the discontinuity between the claim of Jacob b. Yekutiel's settlement in Flanders and any additional attestations of a Jewish presence there. Readers in an earlier period, however, would have certainly been wiser.

But assumptions are not necessary, as another technical issue forcefully proves. In the course of the narrative, Jacob b. Yekutiel offers the pope a bribe. The author of 1007, however, had little faith in venality, and he introduced a bribe sequence specifically to emphasize his belief. Indeed, the bribe plays no evident role in the ultimate papal decision to honor Jacob b. Yekutiel's petition, and, what is more, the amount of the bribe was the paltry sum of 200 pounds. By way of comparison, the Jews of Blois had grossly underestimated the amount needed to bribe Count Thibaut in order to save only thirty-one members of their immediate community from execution in 1171; and their offer was 280 pounds. The sum of 200 pounds, furthermore, barely exceeded the document fee sometimes required by the papal Chancery in return for issuing a text of importance to any petitioner (whether he be Christian, Jew or other).[132]

In any case, the triviality of the bribe is most apparent from 1007 itself. Immediately after offering the bribe, Jacob b. Yekutiel promises a sum far in excess of 200 pounds just to cover the expenses of the bishop-legate who was to journey from place to place bearing the papal letter ordering the cessation of King Robert's persecution.[133] And at this point in the sequence, the author made an anachronistic blunder. Perhaps to add vivifying detail, he specified that the bribe was to consist of 100 pounds Anjou and 100 pounds Limoges. Both coins were of roughly equal value, but what is important here is that both coins were specified together. The Anjou pound, the money of Rouen in the period of Plantagenet rule in the late twelfth century, went out of use in the first quarter of the thirteenth century, with the entry of the Capetians. The Limoges pound was not minted at all until 1211.[134] A bribe specifically composed of these two monies could not, then, have been made before 1211. Of course, the bribe sequence of 1007 might be a later interpolation in an earlier story, but there is nothing in the text to substantiate such a claim. The reference simultaneously to the pounds of Anjou and Limoges, therefore, makes the thirteenth century origin of 1007 definite.

One final point: Were 1007 a product of the eleventh century, the sharp division found in the story between clerical and lay characters, and especially the absence of clerics in the royal entourage, would have been improbable or impossible. The work of J. F. Lemarignier on early Capetian government has revealed the decisive and preponderant role played by bishops in eleventh century royal assemblies and programs.[135]

Conversely, the replacement of clerics by lay officials to form a royal privy council, precisely as depicted in 1007, did not take place before the very late twelfth century.[136]

The Meaning of the "1007 Anonymous"

What then is to be made of all this? Why does the entire story evolve as it does, beginning with a Haman-like conspiracy on the part of the royal lay advisors and nobility to arouse the king against the Jews and continuing with the king charging the Jews by saying

> I have weighed the matter with my ministers and officials, and my desire is to have *one people*—[137]

a oneness he believes so necessary that he willingly uses force to achieve it? Why, too, should all these plans and actions ultimately be checked at the command of the pope and his bishops?

Once the time of 1007's composition is known, the answer to these questions is apparent. The actions and demands attributed to the king and his barons reflect a Jewish recognition that from sometime in the mid-thirteenth century, a transvaluation of meanings had begun to take place in certain spiritual concepts and identities once belonging exclusively to the Church. This transvaluation itself was the product of those fundamental changes in thirteenth century society that Ernst Kantorowicz aptly defined as the "spiritualization and sanctification of the secular." Perhaps most illustrative of this process, the term *corpus mysticum* (the Church itself) was coming to be used with reference to the incipient nation states, and the inhabitants of those states were beginning to see themselves as the *populus dei* (formerly, the body of believers in Christ).[138] Eventually, such usages as the Holy or Chosen Nation, endowed with a divine mission, became regular.[139] And the specific *patria* of the kingdom was on its way to replacing the onetime *patria communis* of the Church.[140]

The effects of this transvaluation process were felt by the Jews both directly and indirectly. Directly, the exchange of meanings also led to an exchange of functions, so that kings soon began interfering in matters once thought to be purely spiritual and ecclesiastical concerns. For example, Louis IX, stopped Jewish lending at interest, and Philip IV, fearing violations of his sovereignty, but also believing it was his proper religious duty, demanded the right to oversee the workings of the papal inquisition in his realm, especially if the defendants were Jews.[141] Indirectly, just as churchmen had once tended to label all dissidence judaizing, so, now, secular authorities began stigmatizing Christian deviants with this term. Edward I's use of "judaizers" to condemn Christian lenders, noted earlier, was borrowed directly from a letter of Bernard of Clairvaux; and, in Bruges, Christian lenders were socially segregated from other Christians in much the same way that Jews were segregated from Christian society as a whole.[142] Such terminology and its underlying attitudes, however, could not but create anxiety about the actions of the Jews themselves. And, on the basis of specific laws in the Theodosian and Justinianic Codes, kings started interjecting themselves into Jewish internal affairs of a purely *Jewish* religious nature.[143]

This royal interference also took place within a new and threatening framework, it too an effect of the transvaluation process. The refusal of the Jew, the enemy of the Gospels,[144] to nullify his distinct identity and make of himself "one people" with the others had come to be confused with an opposition to lay society itself, and to the fledgling body politic of the kingdom in particular. Consequently, large groups of laymen began viewing the stubborn resistence of the Jews to assimilation and amalgamation as synonymous with those forces in the body politic operating against unity, harmony, and religious discipline. This was especially so in the thirteenth century, when those forces, like the undefined relationship between the royal prerogative and the obligation of the king to respect the law, were not as yet fully comprehended. Lay society thus was coming to see the Jews as subversives and in the same symbolic terms once used exclusively by extremist Carolingian clergy. If Jews had once been labelled by Agobard of Lyons as the *impedimentum* preventing the realization of the reformed and perfected ideal Christian society,[145] now, they were designated as the *impedimentum* working against the good of the *patria* and its members, collectively as well as individually. Indeed, in the 1007 narrative, this is precisely what the lay counsellors tell the king, and this is also what pushes him to act. "The Jews," these advisors say, "are an obstacle (*moqesh*)—an *impedimentum*, a snare, and a lure—in our way (to becoming one people);" we must destroy them completely.[146]

Therefore, in the 1007 narrative, as in the *Milḥemet Miṣvah* of Meir b. Simeon, it is the king and his lay advisors who take the lead in "matters of religion." But the ideas in 1007 go beyond those in the *Milḥemet miṣvah*. By pointedly invoking the idea of the Jews an impediment to the formation of a unified people, 1007 was explaining why, by taking the lead in spiritual affairs, the king had become extremely dangerous, and why the Jews had to renounce their old theories and turn elsewhere for security. For it was not piety alone that motivated the king, nor the unembellished Christian theology of the Jewish enemy. Rather, *pro defensione patriae et coronae*[147] the king had harnessed both piety and theology to the imperfect aspirations and the unfathomed mysteries of the emerging territorial states and, with respect to the motives of certain magnates, to the needs of Realpolitik as well. The resulting fusion, in which politics and piety became mutually indistinguishable, was disastrous. It made the king and his followers a greater threat to the Jews than the Church had ever been.[148]

This does not mean that the author of 1007 was urging Jews to turn unhesitatingly to the Church for protection, and to the members of the hierarchy or the pope in particular. Their powers of protection were not unlimited, and this was certainly true of the hierarchy, whose unpredictability and frequent differences of opinion with the papacy the author of 1007 chose to pass over in his concern to counterpoise popes to kings. As for the popes, in the view of 1007, their actions were governed by two determinants: the law and the limits of papal jurisdiction. With regard to the first of these determinants, 1007 considered the popes to be scrupulously consistent. Accordingly, he had the pope in the narrative restate the clauses of *Sicut Iudaeis* and stress the right of the Jews to enjoy due process. For this reason, too, he had the pope ignore a monetary offer, although, as mentioned above, the 200 pounds tendered were surely too little to constitute a serious bribe, and, in fact, may have been only an above-board fee for issuing the bull halting the persecution.

But what was more pressing for 1007 was the second determinant, the limits of papal jurisdiction. Were the popes to exercise the direct jurisdiction over the Jews the Duke of Normandy (in the narrative) conceded them, the enforcement of the safeguards and protections found in Church law would have been guaranteed without exception. However, the exercise of this power would also have insured the rigid application of the body of canons severely defining and limiting Jewish behavior. Direct papal jurisdiction over the Jews, in other words, would have been as disadvantageous as beneficial.

The author of 1007 understood this quite well. Nevertheless, it was a situation he plainly advocated. Thus, addressing the pope, whom he calls the *Apiphior* (as the pope is commonly referred to in Hebrew *after* the beginning of the thirteenth century),[149] Jacob b. Yekutiel says:

> I have found none, save God, who stands above you as a ruler in the lands of the Nations; for you are the Head of the Nations and the ruler over them.

> So I came to cry out about my ills *from the Jews who live under your jurisdiction*. For evil men have arisen without your sanction, and they have attacked the Jews (using force to make them convert to Christianity; which is wrong . . . For) *they* do not have the governance over the Jews to make them leave their Torah . . . That belongs only to the pope of Rome.[150]

The jurisdiction Jacob b. Yekutiel grants the pope, then, is complete. Not only may the pope summon Jews before his courts; he may even make them "abandon their teachings."

This idea of direct papal jurisdiction over the Jews is the key to understanding 1007's purposes. At first glance, it seems to derive from *Sicut Iudaeis* and its clause of conditional protection. But neither this, nor any other clause in the bull confers upon the pope the right to pass judgment over Jewish literature and, in effect, to proscribe Judaism itself. Beyond that, before the thirteenth century, even the canonists did not claim a papal right to exercise direct jurisdiction over non-Christians. At that time, the question of such a right was taken up by Alanus and Hostiensis and, later, by Augustinus Triumphus.[151] An explicit assertion of papal jurisdiction over Jews, however, did not appear until the middle of the century in Innocent IV's *Apparatus* to the *Decretals*.

> *The pope* (Innocent wrote) has jurisdiction and power over all. (Whence), *he may judge Jews*. (He, may do so) if they act contrary to their law in issues of morality, and their own prelates do not punish them, and, equally, *if they fall into heresy with respect to their own law*. (It was) for this reason that popes Gregory IX and Innocent IV ordered their books burned. For they contained many heresies.[152]

It was on the basis of assertions like this and other similar expressions of papal monarchism—of a papal king of kings who rules Christians and infidels alike—that the author of 1007 built his case. Indeed, he must have known these papal claims to direct jurisdiction over infidels and Jews directly. His formulae and those of Innocent IV bear a striking resemblance to each other.

Yet, even more indicative of his knowledge is the gap separating the claims of the papal monarchists from concrete medieval reality. The popes of the thirteenth century, as the author of 1007 incontrovertibly knew, exercised real and direct power over kings only on rare and, usually, troubled occasions. And, as a rule, the popes were hesitant about openly interfering in royal affairs, notwithstanding papal monarchist theories to the contrary.[153] For their part, the kings were loathe to concede jurisdictional rights to ecclesiastical courts, irrespective of the identity, religion or status of the litigants. Nor had things ever been otherwise, especially—one feels compelled to add in view of the supposed origins of 1007—in the early eleventh century. The researches of Pfister, Lemarignier and Foreville have shown that the popes of that period controlled neither the King of France nor the Duke of Normandy. Not even the bishops were in their power. French bishops had rejected decrees imported into France by papal legates on more than one occasion, including, presumably, decrees concerning Jews.[154]

Besides, even if the pope had been all powerful, the fact remains that prior to the thirteenth century and the commentaries of Hostiensis and Innocent IV, papal claims to direct jurisdiction over Jews for any reason and in any sphere were simply non-existent.[155] As late as 1208, Innocent III turned to Philip Augustus and asked his help: "Since compulsion by temporal power may accomplish more among those in the case of whom spiritual compulsion is *not admissible*."[156] The closest thing to direct jurisdiction, the so-called "punishment of the Jews," or "indirect excommunication," threatening Christians with excommunication for maintaining contacts with Jews who had violated the canons, was itself a late innovation. It appeared first in the letters of Innocent III, or possibly Alexander III,[157] and Thomas Aquinas still thought of it as the unique method making direct interference in Jewish affairs and conduct possible.[158]

The point thus seems quite clear: The author of 1007 was writing from the perspective of the most advanced, as well as the most assertive, in mid-thirteenth century papal thought.

This advocacy of extreme papalist theory is puzzling. That theory potentially threatened Jewish existence, as the attack on the Talmud and the permission given the inquisition to deal with Jewish fautors of heresy amply illustrate. Nevertheless, this puzzle is easily resolved by examining Jacob b. Yekutiel's petition to the pope and its results. "Lawless men have arisen," Jacob says, "without your legal sanction, and they have attacked the Jews under your jurisdiction."[159] These "lawless men," of course, were the king and his advisors. The king, in particular, had usurped papal rights. First he had unlawfully demanded that the Jews "reveal to him their knowledge, hiding or obfuscating nothing," and, then, he had compounded his temerity by decreeing a persecution with the aim of creating "one people," since he had found fault with Jewish books and beliefs. But, at this point, the pope correctly stepped in. Following the reasoning of Innocent IV, not to mention 1007 itself, it was the pope alone who had the authority to make the Jews "abandon their teachings." Thus, the pope halted the illegal persecution and cited none other than *Sicut Iudaeis* as the immediate grounds for his action. Jacob b. Yekutiel's petition, in other words, had made hierocratic theory operate to Jewish advantage.

But of what virtue was this ideal scenario of 1007, unless it corresponded to reality? In fact, the 1007 story was not as divorced from reality as it might seem. Leaving aside the issue of papal monarchist theories and their acceptance, and looking at the individual elements of the 1007 narrative, it becomes apparent that its story does closely follow the thrust of thirteenth century royal and papal behavior toward the Jews, especially in England and France. In 1236, for example, Louis IX failed to halt a massacre in Aquitaine, and he did no more at the time of the blood libel at Valreas in 1247.[160] His usury legislation, furthermore, considerably exceeded the limits set down by the canons and papal policy, and was edicted with true animus, as Meir b. Simeon was quick to point out.[161] On one occasion, Louis IX even demanded that the Jews either cease their lending activities forthwith or leave his territories. The clergy, he insisted, might attend to Christian lenders, but it was his royal and moral obligation to stop Jews from taking usury. Under no circumstances would he allow Jews "to infect (his) land with their poison."[162] To insure the execution of his demands, moreover, Louis sent out royal officials, who successfully forced Jews to remit interest that had already been paid.[163] In the face of such pressures, Meir b. Simeon's assertion that by prohibiting the Jews from lending at interest Louis IX was preventing them from observing their faith is quite understandable. Meir's further assertion at this point in his tract, that "the king has unlawfully tried to make us forsake our faith for his,"[164] was no less apt.

The activities of Louis IX were not exceptional. Philip IV expressly followed Louis' usury policies, as did Henry III and Edward I on the other side of the channel.[165] In addition, Philip III and Philip IV, *ad promotionem et defensionem fidei*, and presumably the "common good" as well, adopted the demands of the bull, *Turbato corde*, and allowed the Papal Inquisition to operate against apostate converts and those who aided their return to Judaism.[166] They also went beyond the demands of the bull. Philip III prohibited Jews from living in small towns, where they might pervert *simplices* and seduce them into adopting Judaism, while Philip IV, who shared the concern of his father for Christian *simplices*, on one occasion vowed to stop the horrifying practice of Jews acquiring consecrated wafers, whence *presumpserunt nequiter pertractare Sanctissimum Corpus Christi.*[167] More extreme, Henry III and Edward I executed Jewish victims of blood libels in 1255 and 1276.[168] Magnates too, for reasons that were often as self-serving as pious, were willing to come to legislative understandings with kings when the subject of the legislation was the restraint of Jews—however much they otherwise resented royal manipulations exploiting the Jews at their expense.[169]

The actions of the popes were markedly different. *Turbato corde*, even in its expanded form of 1274, which charges Jews with open proselytizing among born Christians, does not call for Jewish segregation. Nor does it imply, as did Philip III, a collective Jewish subversiveness and threat to society.[170] On the contrary, the record of papal opposition to blood libels and charges of host and cross desecration, as well as to anti-Jewish violence of any kind, is well known.

The correct direction of papal dealings with Jews and the extent of their divergence from royal policies is seen best in the events surrounding the burning of the Talmud at Paris in the 1240s. When all the claims and counterclaims concerning the responsibility for the burning are stripped away, the Bishop of Paris, William of Auvergne, and the University Chancellor and papal legate, Odo of Chateauroux, emerge as the Talmud's major clerical antagonists.[171] Their activities, however, were eventually checked by Innocent IV, even though both he and Gregory IX had initially sanctioned the burnings. Weighing the totality of his obligations, Innocent IV instructed Odo in 1247 to "harm no one *unjustly*" and to "tolerate such (books) as he will find may be tolerated, in accordance with the divine command and without injury to the Christian faith."[172] Instructively, the Talmud had originally been condemned for allegedly causing such injury through its supposed mocking of Christianity and its falsifying of the true law of Moses.[173] The pope, therefore, had not merely changed his mind or yielded to pressures and bribes. Innocent IV's edict of 1247 was based on principle: The Jews could not be treated "unjustly." His stance, moreover, was firm. Not even the signatures of forty-four leading Parisian masters and clergy gathered by Odo in 1248 were able to reverse it.[174] In fact, the principles of just treatment and due process underlying the decision to tolerate certain Jewish books may be seen repeatedly and thematically in many other letters Innocent IV issued concerning Jews.[175]

In contrast, the policies of Louis IX made him into a true enemy of the Talmud. Not only did he take an active role in the first round of examinations and burnings, but, in 1254, he overrode Innocent IV's 1247 decision and prohibited all use and study of the Talmud.[176] Quite possibly, the author of 1007 was referring to just these actions when he wrote that in the council of his barons and at the urging of his queen, the king questioned the legitimacy of the practice of Judaism and demanded of the Jews that they reveal to him their knowledge, "hiding or obfuscating nothing." It was these actions, too, that brought 1007 into full agreement with the opinion of Meir b. Simeon: The king indeed did think he knew more of religion than the pope himself.[177]

In the policies of kings and popes, therefore, the author of 1007 had seen a pattern. The popes were seeking—albeit by understatement and implication—to put into practice certain elements of extreme hierocratic theory. One of these elements was the claim to jurisdiction over the Jews in matters of belief. Specifically, the popes were asserting their exclusive right to supervise the purity of Judaism by deciding what was correct or heretical in current Jewish practice,[178] by dictating, for example, which parts of their Talmudic learning and knowledge the Jews must put aside. Nevertheless, the popes tempered this claim, and others like it, by assiduously observing the law and due legal process. Indeed, in all of papal thought, the matters of jurisdiction, legal rigor, and due process were consciously and inextricably linked.[179] The kings, in contrast, knew of no such theories, and, often, they were unwilling to acknowledge the limitations of the law. Hence, as a source of protection, the pope was clearly preferable to the king.

But this protection would be even more efficient if papal monarchist and jurisdictional claims concerning the Jews were ubiquitously accepted, and not only on a random basis when they suited royal interests—which is what had happened with the Talmud. If reality as a whole, that is, and not simply its isolated and individual elements, were to correspond to the 1007 narrative, the Jews would benefit inestimably.

Yet, how could such a thing come about? As the author of 1007 knew, reality would never reflect his narrative perfectly. Royal opposition to papal monarchism, for one thing, was continually increasing. Nevertheless, opposition to papal monarchism was not synonymous with opposition to the papacy as an institution or to its generally acknowledged rights in spiritual affairs. Kings would always be most hesitant to meddle in these matters. Thus, Philip IV, together with his royal propagandists, claimed it was part of the royal prerogative to initiate judicial proceedings against heretics. Even so, preferring not to interfere with tradition, Philip pressed the pope, Clement V, to take the initiative in prosecuting the Templars.[180] Against this background, the author of 1007 had reason to be optimistic. Should the Jews come to understand papal doctrines, along with the overall theoretical underpinnings of the thirteenth century world, then perhaps they might persuade the popes to insist on the practical implementation of those jurisdictional prerogatives over the Jews and Judaism the papacy had heretofore claimed only in theory.

The 1007 was composed to instill this understanding. Jews had to be taught a number of lessons. First, they had to learn that the canons defining their role in the Christian world order were all equivocal and highly complex in nature. Second, they had to appreciate that in principle the pope—although not every member of the clergy—was committed to observing punctiliously the entire body of canon law, irrespective of whom a particular canon favored or limited, be he Christian or Jew. Third, and most important, the Jews had to understand that the popes had enunciated in theory that as the legatee of Peter, the papacy had every right to supervise the implementation of the canons pertaining to the Jews. In this task, moreover, royalty was to follow the papal lead. It was not to dictate it.

Such knowledge would not enable the Jews to control the pope. Nor, of course, would the Jews ever admit the legitimacy of the potentially destructive power claimed by the pope to judge their religious activities and their literature in particular. The whole question of papal monarchism and its theory was significant for Jews only insofar as it impinged on reality, affecting their lives; in their hearts, the pope was none other than the supreme representative of an idolatrous faith.[181] The Jews, however, could learn what the powers the pope claimed over them and their faith were, and, equally important, they could learn how the pope intended to use these powers in the light of the canons regulating the Jewish-Christian encounter. Only then, through the use of this knowledge and not through venality and other such traditional, but ineffective "personal" approaches could the Jews hope to convince the pope to republish the texts and demand the implementation of their canonically guaranteed rights—even in the face of royal opposition.

In the absence of this sophistication, the Jews would not be able to defend themselves, and this was especially so in the light of the new challenges that arose in the later thirteenth century. As noted above, various pressures, but primarily the concern over enforcing the canons prohibiting apostasy after baptism,[182] persuaded the popes of this period to invoke their theories of direct jurisdiction over Jews and issue bulls like *Turbato corde* directing the Papal Inquisition to summon Jews before it on charges of aiding and abetting heretics and of helping Jews who had once converted return to their original faith.[183]

This does not mean every contact between the Inquisition and the Jews led ineluctably to a judicial lynching. At times, Jews and accused judaizers were acquitted.[184] And a close reading of the famous transcript of the trial of Baruch (ca. 1322) shows the Inquisitor-Bishop, Jacques Fournier (later, Benedict XII), seeking over and over to prove that at some point Baruch had expressed his will to convert; whence, both the conversion, as well as Fournier's current inquisitorial proceedings would be vindicated as wholly legal.[185] Still, extremist inquisitors could exploit judaizing activities—in other words, violations of the contractual terms of canons like *Sicut Iudaeis* and *Dispar nimirum* demanding Jewish subservience—as a pretext for demanding such actions as a new general confiscation of whatever Hebrew books the Jews had managed to preserve.[186] The only way to avoid this catastrophe, not to mention the encroachment of the Inquisition into all spheres of Jewish life, was to know the law in intimate detail. Jews had to know not only where to turn for legal redress, but also how to do so.

This assessment of Jewish security prospects was not arrived at easily. Some Jews were perplexed about papal activity; to them, it did not appear to fit into a consistent scheme or pattern. Natan Official, the author of the *Debate of Rabbi Yehiel of Paris* (concerning the "errors" of the Talmud), was so unsure that he left his readers wondering. At one point, the Queen tells the rabbi that the pope has ordered the Talmud put on trial. But near the end of the tract, the pope is proclaimed a safe and sure protector.[187] What Natan Official missed, although the author of 1007 did not, was that all of papal policy toward the Jews moved simultaneously in two directions: one offering protection, the other threatening violators of the canons with the loss of their privileges. Perceived within this dualistic framework, the papal claim to judge the orthodoxy of Jewish texts—and Innocent IV's bifurcated approach to the Talmud, in particular—are easily understood; indeed, Innocent IV had no *permissible* alternative.

This full grasp of papal ways displayed by the author of 1007 was soon to become widespread. At the request of the Spanish Dominicans, Clement IV wrote to James I of Aragon in 1266, asking the King to punish Nahmanides for circulating a blasphemous work following his 1263 disputation with Paul Christian at Barcelona. In the heart of Clement's letter, however, the terms of *Sicut Iudaeis* are effectively reiterated.[188] James I is told to protect Christianity and repress Jewish malice wherever it appears; yet, he must do so without violating those privileges the Apostolic See has bestowed upon the Jews. This admonition was certainly not drafted in response to a Dominican request. More than likely, it was the product of a carefully worded petition to the pope on the part of a Jewish delegation seeking to limit the effects of the Dominican threat.

Jews became adept petitioners. Petitions led, for example, to their inclusion in edicts rebuking Inquisitors for sidestepping legal propriety and dragging defendants to distant venues for trial.[189] Three such edicts were even issued by a former General of the Franciscan Order, Nicholas IV (Girolamo Masci). On another occasion, a petition may have been responsible for the assurances given in 1298 to the Jews of Pamiers by the Dominican Inquisitor, Arnold Dejean (although here, it should be noted, Dejean was also the feudal lord of the town). Customary privileges, Dejean promised, would be respected and no threatening innovations introduced.[190] When petitioned, therefore, even the Inquisition could be made to respect the limits ordained by the canons and the popes.

The example of these petitions shows that 1007 did not stand alone. Others too came to understand the truths of papal theory and power, and they sought to make this knowledge work to Jewish advantage.[191] Perhaps the best illustration of this point comes from the pronouncements made by the Jewish assembly meeting at Barcelona in 1354.[192] A petition, the assembly specified, was to be delivered to the pope. Preferably, this petition was to be transmitted through the agency of Pedro IV of Aragon, but, if necessary, the king was to be by-passed and representatives sent directly to Clement VI at Avignon. There, the pope would be pressed to issue a decretal letter denouncing host libels, accusations of well-poisoning, and all legislation going beyond that of the canons limiting Jewish behavior during Holy Week. The pope would also be urged to restrict the activities of the Inquisition, primarily, by enforcing the edict of Boniface VIII insisting that inquisitors not treat Jews as "powerful persons." The identity of those who brought accusations and gave witness against them could not be kept a secret.[193] Finally, the pope was to be confronted with the following: In an explicit echo of the *Apparatus* of Innocent IV, on the one hand, and with the implication that *Turbato corde* ought to be modified, on the other, the assembly instructed its representatives to admit the right of the Inquisition to judge Jews erring in beliefs common to all. But these representatives were also to argue the illegality of inquisitional proceedings against Jews expressing opinions true to Judaism, even if these opinions somehow stimulated the growth of Christian heresy. The pope, the assembly then concluded, is obligated to agree to all of these requests, for he is bound to uphold the laws and teachings of Christianity—including those demanding the preservation of the Jews.

The declaration made at the 1274 Council of Lyons by the Imperial publicist, Alexander of Roes, may thus have been intended as more than hyperbole.

> Not only, (he wrote), did the Christian people and ecclesiastical prelates assemble at the feet of the Roman pontiff, but even the kings of the world,

> *together with the Jews*, Greeks and Tartars, confessed that the monarchy of the world (belonged) to the Roman Priest.[194]

It was in this same spirit, although considerably later, in the sixteenth century, that Solomon Modena, half fawningly, yet still earnestly declared:

> Behold . . . from him (the pope) a law (literally, Torah) will go out and a religion to the entire world . . . .[195]

The Esoteric Approach of the "1007 Anonymous"

But why did the author of 1007 state his case esoterically? Perhaps he was afraid, fearing the wrath of some king, possibly St. Louis himself, who was credited by his contemporary biographer with the apophthegm: The best way to argue with a Jew is with a sword in the belly.[196] More centrally, 1007 could not hope that a formal lecture on canonical procedure and theory would yield positive results. He could not delude himself into thinking he could convince his fellow Jews by saying: Go before the pope, as did Jacob b. Yekutiel, flatter him by spouting papal monarchism, tell him that you accept his claim to jurisdiction over non-believers, that you concede unequivocally his right to review and expurgate your sacred texts and traditions, and that you see the canons with their whole panoply of restrictions as establishing valid norms for Jewish life, literature and religious practices. Nor could he persuade the Jews to pretend that in doing all this they were not demeaning and humiliating themselves. For how, after all, could he tell the Jews outright that if they wanted papal help, they must be ready to live according to the canonical demands of subservient inferiority, trusting that in return for their acquiescence, the pope would honor his canonically attested pledge to afford them due legal process? To say this would be calling divine providence and God's promise to His People into question.

The prescription, therefore, was too extreme; it had to be masked and made palatable. Yet, somehow, it had to be communicated. For the dilemma the Jews faced was not a simple one in which they had only to choose between kings and popes. Nor, as the author of 1007 correctly perceived, was crafty maneuvering effective. What the Jews had to learn was why kings were dangerous. And, even more, they had to be taught the prerequisites for receiving papal support. There was room for neither despair nor euphoria, but only for the level-headed appraisal of reality and theory.

This whole program was terrifying to contemplate. It also left certain problems unresolved. As the author of 1007 knew, papal decrees were effective only when secular authorities cooperated. In the long run, however, the normative ecclesiastical sources—the popes and the clergy who adhered fully to the canons—did not receive this cooperation. For reasons of politics and piety, kings and nobles could, and would, be more rigid than the canons demanded and more ruthless than even Agobard of Lyons had dreamed. In the face of such opposition, the popes had to act accordingly. Despite their claims, they rarely, if ever, insisted on exercising direct jurisdiction over Jews in practice. Thus, rather than interfering directly in Jewish religious affairs, in 1248, Innocent IV still preferred resorting to "indirect excommunication" to halt violations of Jewish clothing regulations.[197] Here, as in the case of the Talmud, the pope felt it politic to turn to the community of Christians and to the secular powers for enforcement. He could not cavalierly deliver a direct order as though no intermediary stood between him and the Jews.

There was also the nagging, and closely related, question of how forcefully any given pope was committed to speaking out in the cause of Jewish defense and thereby chancing a blow to the prestige of his own pontificate, as well as to that of the papal office as a whole. The papal commitment in principle to law and due legal process was, in practice, vulnerable to harsh realities. If the King of England expelled his Jews, to the accompaniment of much popular acclaim, the pope could not afford to call openly for the revocation of the expulsion decree. It would have never been revoked; and the papacy would have been severely embarrassed. The pope might have tried to mollify his personal sense of justice by claiming that the permission given Jews to dwell in Christian lands did not imply a right to dwell in those lands universally. But his primary decision to remain silent would have been politically motivated and self-serving. Following the expulsion from England in 1290, therefore, Nicholas IV did not speak out.

Apart from problems caused by external factors, papal Jewry policy suffered from a serious internal flaw. For all its attempts to be consistent, it was plagued by scores of inherent contradictions. Sometimes, these contradictions were obvious. The protection offered by *Sicut Iudaeis* was jeopardized by the prosecution threatened by *Turbato corde*. Yet, so visible a clash was generally controllable, as, for instance, in the letters of Nicholas IV, mentioned above, warning Inquisitors against excessive zeal. Real problems arose when the contradictions were more complex and especially when they grew out of legal overdefinition and refinement. Thus, *Vineam sorec* (1278) urges sermons of a missionary nature. But since these sermons smack of possible forced conversion, the bull ends on a surprisingly weak note. Instead of excommunicating Christian violators of its edicts and threatening recalcitrant Jews with "indirect excommunication," the bull merely requests a report be made to the pope, Nicholas III, who will then consider taking "appropriate (disciplinary) measures."[198]

The case of *Vineam sorec* was not unique. A Latin transcript of Jewish origin, describing the reissue of *Sicut Iudaeis* to the Jews of Pamplona around 1280, explained that the bull was dispatched to deal with the problem of Franciscans delivering (missionary) sermons and interrupting Jewish prayers. These interruptions were to cease; for while the sermons were beneficial, the prayers, like Judaism itself, were protected by the canons.[199]

The ambivalence of this Pamplona episode must have left both Franciscans and Jews in a quandry. The popes were dealing with reality on too theoretical a plane. Furthermore, the distinctions into which theory led the popes sometimes created untenable situations. In approximately 1266, Clement IV wrote of the plight of a seven year old Jewish girl baptized under dubious circumstances and ordered her returned to her father, who "was being tormented by fatherly emotions." Yet, he also noted the agreement of the father ultimately to restore his daughter to the Church, since the sacrament of baptism could not be invalidated. The father, obviously, was supposed to raise his daughter as a Christian—which, of course, was preposterous. This compromise had as little chance of being realized as the story, told by the twelfth-century Caesarius of Heisterbach, of the refusal of a young baptized Jewess to return to her father may be considered authentic.[200]

Scrupulous adherence to the law on the part of the popes, therefore, was not always a direct path to safety and security. Accordingly, writers like Meir b. Simeon cautioned against relying on the popes exclusively. Meir was too aware of papal limitations to be overly positive. But the author of 1007 was no less aware. It was he, after all, who had spoken of the papal right to force the Jews from their teachings. Yet, he saw no viable alternative. For if Meir b. Simeon had referred to the Code of the Emperor as a possible source of security, the author of 1007 knew that Meir was only being hopeful. The truth was that for all his vulnerability, for all the legal overdefinitions and the resulting ambivalences, and for all the limitations he placed on his protection, the pope, in the long run, was infinitely more reliable and absolutely more consistent than his weak and vacillating imperial counterpart. The Jews had no choice but to call on the pope actively.

Yet, in the final analysis, the confidence the author of 1007 placed in the pope was not the product of careful reasoning and calculation. It was the product of his belief that papal-Jewish relations were determined by a divinely preordained pattern. Jacob b. Yekutiel, therefore, appears as a latter-day Mordechai, whose boldness and cunning save the Jews from a ministerial plot. The real prototype of Jacob b. Yekutiel, however, was not Mordechai, but Ehud ben Gerah (Judges 3). The crucial private interview granted Jacob b. Yekutiel by the pope is a pure retelling of the events leading to Ehud's seclusion with Eglon, the King of Moab, on Eglon's attic—except that all the elements are presented in perfect contraposition. In both cases, the excuse for the privacy is the enticement: "I have a secret to tell you" (Judges 3:19). But in the case of Ehud, that secret is the "two-edged sword" with which he slays Eglon and brings about the flight of the Moabite persecutors. In the case of Jacob b. Yekutiel, it is the message to the pope that he is the Vicar of Christ, empowered to rule over the Jews, which prompts the order halting the royally instigated pogrom. By implication, therefore, the kingdom of Eglon was evil (*memshelet zadon*—indeed, in the story, that of Robert of France is referred to as *malkhut harish^c ah*), the kingdom of the pope, the "King of the nations," just (*memshelet reshut*). The heavy yoke of this kingdom, including the Perpetual Servitude[201] it had ordained, could thus, at least temporarily, be borne.

Medieval Jewish readers would not have missed the parallelism between these two stories, nor would they have missed the message the author of 1007 hoped to convey to them through it. They may have also sensed another parallel, but this one not even the author of 1007 dared make except by allusion. If, at God's behest, the slavery (Judges 3:14) to Eglon had ended, then, at the time of God's choosing, that to the pope too would also cease. When, therefore, the author of 1007 wrote of a miracle preventing the execution of Jacob b. Yekutiel in Rouen and convincing the Duke of Normandy to send Jacob on his mission, he was serious indeed. Without the faith that all of this, the miracle, the papal intervention, and even *Sicut Iudaeis* and the body of canons regulating Jewish behavior, was of divine making, then even he, the realist and tactician, would likely have given up all hope and become a Christian—as did a not inconsiderable number of his contemporaries.[202]

In Conclusion

The positive attitude revealed by Ephraim of Bonn toward the popes and the Church hierarchy was thus justified. But this attitude had to mature and be converted into the elements of an operative strategy before it could be of real use. That maturational process reached its completion in the 1007 Anonymous. Its author accurately perceived that in the century between 1150 and 1250, the papacy and the canonists had elaborated on the fundamentals set forth in *Dispar nimirum* and *Sicut Iudaeis*. In bulls, councils and canonical collections, rules had been carefully defined governing papal-Jewish relations. Thenceforth, the Church would insist on the scrupulous enforcement of these rules, to the Jews' advantage and disadvantage alike.[203] The Jews had to know, therefore, precisely where they stood. Through knowledge and deliberate action, the basic privileges of life and the right to practice Judaism freely could be asserted; and these privileges would be guaranteed, to the best of his ability, by the pope himself.[204]

This strategy was meaningless, however, if the canons delineating papal policy were not functional and their authority continually challenged. But challenged it was, and the papal Jewry policy mandating a specific and necessary role for the Jews in Christian society ultimately failed. One by one, and against everything the popes and churchmen like Augustine and Bernard of Clairvaux had said or written, the Jews were partially or totally expelled from every Western European state. For reasons of economics, politics, constitutional weakness, social conflict or piety, singly or in fusion—perhaps verbalized as the desire, so perceptively sensed by 1007, to be "one people"—it was decided to ignore the teachings of the popes and to disregard the determinations of the canons. Indeed, challenged by such a coordinated will, on occasion, the popes themselves had no choice but to abandon the ideal of due legal process and make their peace with political realism.

In the matter of the Jews and their place in the Christian world order, therefore, one of the central difficulties of the medieval world, the establishment of a fully functioning body of canon law and the subsequent division of jurisdictions between lay and ecclesiastical competences, is revealed in the fullness of its complexity and irresolution.[205] So too, the depths of lay piety and its independence from ecclesiastical controls may be fairly measured.

Notes

[1] On modern attitudes toward the popes, see the works cited in K. R. Stow, "The Church and the Jews, From St. Paul to Paul IV," *Bibliographical Essays in Medieval Jewish Studies* (New York, 1976), pp. 107–65, and esp. pp. 124–28, and in my forthcoming "The Church and Neutral History," (in Hebrew) *Jewish Historiography and World History* (Mercaz Shazar, Jerusalem). See also, Shlomo Simonsohn, "Prolegomena to a History of the Relations between the Papacy and the Jews in the Middle Ages," (in Hebrew) *I. F. Baer Memorial Volume, Zion* 44 (1979): 66–93; and Solomon Grayzel, "Popes, Jews and Inquisition—from '*Sicut*' to '*Turbato*'," *Essays on the Occasion of the Seventieth Anniversary of the Dropsie University* (Phila., 1979), pp. 151–88. For a fuller discussion of the theological underpinnings of papal policy, see K. R. Stow, "Hatred of the Jews or Love of the Church: Papal Policy Toward the Jews" (in Hebrew), *Antisemitism Through the Ages*, ed., S. Almog (Jerusalem, 1980), pp. 91–111.

[2] *Pugio Fidei* (Leipzig, 1687), Part III, chap. 21, par. 22, and chap. 23, pars. 1–6; and see R. Bonfil, "The Nature of Judaism in Raymundus Martini's *Pugio Fidei*" (in Hebrew), *Tarbiz* 40 (1971): 360–75.

[3] Cited in J. D. Mansi, *Sacrorum Conciliorum Collectio* (Venice, 1779–82), 59 vols. 24:115; and the 1254 Chapter General cited in E. Martène and U. Durand, *Thesaurus novus anecdotorum* (Paris, 1717), 4: 1706–1708.

[4] A. M. Haberman, *Sefer Gezerot Ṣarfat Ve-ʾAshkenaz* (Jerusalem, 1971), p. 116.

[5] H. H. Ben Sasson, "La-megamah ha-Kronografiah ha-Yehudit shel Yeme ha-Beinayim," *Ha-Historyon Ve-Askolot ha-Historiah* (Jerusalem, 1963), pp. 29–49.

[6] On the bull, *Sicut Iudaeis*, and on its origins, see below. The text published by Eugenius III was first issued by Calixtus II ca. 1120.

[7] Haberman, *Sefer Gezerot*, pp. 24–60. See S. W. Baron, *A Social and Religious History of the Jews*, 17 vols. (Phila., 1952–1980), 4:288, n. 9 and nn. 17 and 18, for the debate on the date of this text.

[8] See, e.g. Albert of Aix in Martin Bouquet, *Recueil des Historiens des Croisades, Historiens Occidentaux.* (Paris, 1879), 4:292.

[9] Cf. below on Henry IV and Wibert of Ravenna.

[10] Haberman, *Sefer Gezerot*, p. 121. Bernard's remarks on usury are found in J. P. Migne *Patrologia Latina*, 182:568A, letter No. 363.

[11] In J. Müller, *Teshuvot Hakhme Ṣarfat Ve-Lotair* (Vienna, 1881), No. 34, p. 206, who argues for later 12th century France. Irving Agus in *Jewish Quarterly Review* 48 (1957): 95 and Samuel Kraus in *Revue des Etudes Juives (REJ)* 34 (1897): 238, argue for the eleventh century, which is doubtful because of the use of the term "Head of the Bishops," on which see the continuation here. Agus' claim of an Italian locus for the events is interesting and might allow a date ca. 1100.

[12] The unpaid remainder of the debt then becomes the subject of the Responsum itself, which handles principally questions of partnerships and oaths. It should be noted that the

text does not specify the bishop's reaction and that the local ruler supervises the repayment. But it is obvious from the events that either the bishop accepted the papal ruling or else there is a break in the logic of the story.

[13] K. F. Morrison, *Tradition and Authority in the Western Church, 300–1140* (Princeton, 1969), pp. 259–66 and 281–91; and H. E. J. Cowdrey, "Pope Gregory VII and the Anglo-Norman Church and Kingdom," *Studi Gregoriani* 9 (1972): 83 and 96, on Gregory's claims to the headship of all bishops.

[14] Solomon Grayzel, "Pope Alexander III and the Jews," *Salo W. Baron Jubilee Volume* (Jerusalem, 1975), pp. 561–62, and Walter Holtzmann, "Zur paepstlichen Gesetzgebung ueber die Juden in 12ten Jahrhundert," *Festschrift Guido Kisch* (Stuttgart, 1955), p. 229, for the text.

[15] Grayzel, *XIIIth Century*, p. 268, no. 115.

[16] The letter was published by Abraham Harkavy in *Ha-Kedem* 3 (1912): 111–114 and see the comments with selections from the text in Jacob Mann, *Texts and Studies* (reprint New York, 1972), 1: 422–23; Mann dates the letter 1288–92, p. 423.

[17] Obviously, one must distinguish between use by Christians, and even exploitation, on the one hand, and praise, together with threats to the *Guide*'s detractors, on the other: see here, J. I. Dienstag, "St. Thomas Aquinas in Maimonidian Scholarship," in *Studies in Maimonides and St. Thomas Aquinas* (New York, 1975): 192–206.

[18] The most thorough discussion remains Petrus Browe, *Die Judenmission im Mittelalter und die Paepste* (Rome, 1942). Cf. more recently, the extreme theory of Jeremy Cohen, *The Friars and the Jews*, (Ithaca, 1982).

[19] For a translation of Gregory's letter, see Edward Synan, *The Popes and the Jews in the Middle Ages* (New York, 1965), p. 46, citing *Monumenta Germaniae Historica* (*MGH*, *Epist.*) *Epistolarum*, VIII, 25, vol. II, p. 27. The clause of particular interest states: "Sicut iudaeis non debet esse licentia quicquam in synagogis suis ultra quam permissum est lege praesumere, ita in his quae eis concessa sunt nullum debent praeiudicio sustinere . . ." For other letters of Gregory concerning Jews, see Bernhard Blumenkranz, *Les auteurs Chrétiens Latins du Moyen Age sur les Juifs et le Judaisme* (Paris, 1963), pp. 73–86.

[20] *Decretals* of Gregory IX: X.5,6,9, based on the text issued by Clement III (1187–91), which was essentially identical to its predecessors; and see Solomon Grayzel, "The Papal Bull *'Sicut Iudaeis'*" in *Studies and Essays in Honor of Abraham A. Neuman* (Leiden, 1962), pp. 243–80, for a complete history of the bull, as well as for changes introduced by Innocent III, yet not included in the *Decretals* text.

[21] For Stephen III, see J. P. Migne, *Patrologia Latina* (PL), 129: 857. Cf. Hadrian I, comparing iconclasts to Jews, PL 96: 1232, and Leo VII, obliquely calling Judaizing, i.e. feasting on the Sabbath, a heresy, PL 98: 335 (and see Blumenkranz, *Auteurs*, p. 142 and 219–20); and Gregory IV, citing the Fourth Toledan Council on the subject of forcing Jews to remain Christians, even if, illegally, they had been forcibly baptized in the first place, in Gratian, *Decretum*, D.45, c. 5 (cited in Synan, *The Popes*, p. 218).

[22] Agobard's letters on the Jews appear in *MGH Epist. Karolini Aevi*, III, E. Deummler, pp. 164–66 and 179–201. See here Manfred Kneiwasser, "Bischof Agobard von Lyon und der Platz der Juden in Einer Sakral Verfassten Einheits Gesellschaft," *Kairos* 19 (1979): 203–27. For Agobard's school, Bernhard Blumenkranz, "Deux compilations Canoniques de Florus de Lyon et l'action antijuive d'Agobard," *Revue Historique de Droit Français et Êtranger* 33 (1955): 227–54 and 560–62.

[23] See Blumenkranz, *Auteurs*, pp. 177 ff., 228 ff., 237 ff., 264 and 265 ff.; and J. F. Benton, ed., *Self and Society in Medieval France* (New York, 1970), pp. 134–37 and 209–11, for the twelfth century developments on this theme, of a pornographic nature, in the writings of Guibert of Nogent.

[24] For a discussion of such charters, Vittore Colorni, *Legge Ebraica e Leggi Locali* (Milan, 1945), pp. 11–99, and esp. 23–30.

[25] Agobard's differences with Louis the Pious are self-evident from Agobard's letters. On the continuing clash between royal and clerical interests over Jews after Agobard, most sharply at the Diet of Epernay, see Blumenkranz, *Juifs et Chrétiens dans le Monde Occidental* (Paris, 1960), pp. 300–306, and *idem, Auteurs*, p. 208. Yet, see Walter Ullmann, "Public Welfare and Social Legislation in the Early Medieval Councils," *Studies in Church History* 7 (1971): 23, on early medieval royal legislation preventing Jews from holding public offices. The thorny problem of Visigothic Spain, universally conceded to be unique, has been omitted from consideration here. For general problems between kings and clergy, see K. F. Morrison, *The Two Kingdoms, Ecclesiology in Carolingian Political Thought* (Princeton, 1964), and W. Ullmann, *The Carolingian Renaissance and the Idea of Kingship* (London, 1969).

[26] See, e.g., the 1084 Charter of Rudiger of Spire in J. Aronius, *Regesten zur Geschichte der Juden in Frankischen und Deutschen Reiche bis zum Jahre 1273* (Berlin, 1902), p. 69, and of Henry IV, *ibid.*, pp. 71–77.

[27] For the use of this term (and others like it: e.g. *tanquam servi* and *servi regis*), see the texts published in Latin with Hebrew translation and references to original editions by Haim Beinart, *Kitve Zekhuyot Klalliyot shel Yehudei Eiropah* (Jerusalem, 1972), pp. 20–23. On the legal aspects of Chamber Serfdom, see Guido Kisch, *The Jews in Medieval Germany*, 2nd ed. (New York, 1970), pp. 119–28, and pp. 139–53; and cf. Gavin Langmuir, "'*Judei Nostri*' and the Beginnings of Capetian Legislation," *Traditio* 16 (1963): pp. 203–69. In a recent article "*Tanquam Servi*: The Change in Jewish Status in French Law About 1200," in M. Yardeni, ed., *Les Juifs dans l'Histoire de France* (Leiden, 1980): 24–54, Langmuir argues that the legal status of the Jew was so special that Chamber Serfdom, or any other kind of serfdom recalling actual serfdom, is not an applicable term or category, at least not in England or France. Rather, Jews were legally *Judaei*, and nothing more—fully dependent on the King or certain important barons.

[28] See J. C. Holt, *Magna Carta* (Cambridge, 1965), *passim*; and Wm. Stubbs, *Select Charters* (Oxford, 1962), pp. 339, 344, 353, 365, 416 and 487 for thirteenth century charter confirmations. An informative, if not complete parallel appears in Shelomo ibn Verga's *Shebet Yehudah*. See chap. 10, p. 54 of Azriel Shohat's edition (Jerusalem, 1956), where Cardinal Gil Albornoz counsels Gonzalo Martinez de Oviedo against urging Alfonso XI to expel the Jews. Since, says Albornoz, the Jews belong to the King and are a treasure to him, "You are not an enemy of the Jews but of the King (if you counsel expulsion)." See the discussion of this passage in Y. H. Yerushalmi, *The Lisbon Massacre of 1506 and the Royal Image in the Shebet Yehudah* (Cincinnati, 1976), p. 41.

[29] See Robert Chazan, *Medieval Jewry in Northern France* (Baltimore, 1973), pp. 100 ff. on St. Louis; and Gavin Langmuir "The Jews and the Archives of Angevin England," *Traditio* 19 (1963): 183–244, on the problems of piety on all levels of society and the attitudes taken toward Jews; and see the works cited in note 139 below for additional bibliography.

[30] Cecil Roth, *A History of the Jews in England* (Oxford, 1949), p. 102.

[31] On this term and its association with the growing self-consciousness and spiritual aura of the later medieval kingdom, see Gaines Post, "Two Notes on Nationalism in the Middle Ages," *Traditio* 9 (1953): 281–320, esp. 290.

[32] On the legal problems connected with expulsion in the Middle Ages, and also for contemporary opinions on this issue, see Marquardus de Susannis, *De Iudaeis et Aliis Infidelibus* (Venice, 1558), Part I, chap. 7, par. 1. For a further discussion of the Jew in the emerging medieval state, see below.

[33] See S. A. Singer, "The Expulsion of the Jews from England in 1290," *Jewish Quarterly Review* 55 (1964): 117–35, which reviews fully the multiplicity of motifs possibly responsible for expulsions of the Jews. For specifically political aspects of expulsions, as well as problems involving kings and nobility, see M. Kriegel, "Mobilisation Politique et Modernisation Organique," Archives de Sciences Sociales 46 (1978): 5–20.

[34] See Yerushalmi, *Lisbon Massacre*, passim.

[35] Paul in Romans 9–11; Augustine in *Adversus Iudaeos*, passim and see Bernhard Blumenkranz, *Die Judenpredigt Augustins* (Basle, 1946).

[36] See his Eight Orations against the Jews in Migne, *Patrologia Graeca* 48, 843–947; see too, R. L. Wilkens and W. A. Meeks, *Jews and Christians in Antioch in the First Four Centuries of the Common Era* (Missoula, 1978). On those who thought like Chrysostom, and on the clerical desire to expel Jews or use force in converting them, see Petrus Browe, *Die Judenmission im Mittelalter und die Paepste* (Rome, 1942), pp. 13–45, 71–85, and 215–52; on the use of force in conversion, in particular, see Yitzhak Baer, *A History of the Jews in Christian Spain* (Phila., 1966), vol. II, 95–98; and see especially Renata Segre, "Bernardino da Feltre; i Monti di pietà e i banchi ebraici," *Rivista Storica Italiana* 90 (1978): 818–33, for a vivid fifteenth century example of this desire.

[37] See Romans, 11:15–26; Augustine, *The City of God*, Bk. 20, ch. 30; and *The Catechism of the Council of Trent*, trans. J. Donovan, (New York, 1929), p. 64; and cf. Agobard's citation of Romans 11 in *Monumenta Germaniae Historica, Epistolae Karolini Aevi* III, p. 198, and see too p. 184.

[38] This point is seen especially well (to be sure, it must appear in any discussion of the Gregorian Reform) in Gerhard Ladner, "The Concepts of '*Ecclesia*' and '*Christianitas*'. Their Relation to the Idea of Papal '*plenitudo potestatis*' from Gregory VII to Boniface VIII," *Sacerdozio e Regno da Gregorio VII a Bonifacio VIII* (Rome, 1954), passim, and esp. p. 56 for his apt term, "inverted Carolingianism."

[39] The reference here is to S. W. Baron's "'Plenitude of Apostolic Powers' and Medieval 'Jewish Serfdom'", in *Ancient and Medieval Jewish History* (New Brunswick, N.J., 1972), pp. 284–307.

[40] The text of the main letter is found in PL, 146: 1386–1387: Dispar nimirum est Judaeorum et Sarracenorum causa. In illos enim qui Christianos persequuntur et ex urbibus et propriis sedibus pellunt, iuste pugnatur; hi, vero, ubique parati sunt servire." The edited canon is Gratian, *Decretum*, C. 23, q. 8, c. 11; and see the unedited letter in Synan, *The Popes*, p. 218; Alexander II also issued a letter to the Prince of Benevento in 1065 admonishing him for his lack of restraint and use of force in converting Jews. The circumstances which produced this letter were probably akin to those about to be described below for the letters of 1063. For this 1065 text, see Samuel Loewenfeld, *Epistolae Pontificum Romanorum ineditae* (Leipzig, 1885), p. 52, n. 105. On the legal history of the notion of Jewish passivity and toleration through the 16th century, see K. R. Stow, *Catholic Thought and Papal Jewry Policy* (New York, 1977), pp. 104 and 118.

[41] C.T., 16, 8, 18 and 22; cf. with the "Pact of Omar," a generic name for numerous stipulations, dating from no later than the 9th century for regulating Jewish life in the Islamic world; see, e.g. the text in J. R. Marcus, *The Jew in The Medieval World* (New York, 1965), pp. 13–15: "If we violate any of the conditions of this agreement, then we forfeit your protection, and you are at liberty to treat us as enemies and rebels." See, too, Synan, *The Popes*, pp. 53–54, who first pointed to the parallel between The Pact and The Code. The reliance of Islam on Roman Law and the later borrowings from Islamic Jewry Law by the Fourth Lateran Council has, in distinction, long been known. These legal parallels between Islamic and Christian law concerning tolerated non-believers actually

run quite deep. Similarly, the use by Mohammed of such theological terms, common to Christian texts, as deaf, blind, and stiffnecked (See, e.g., The Quran, Sura II), to describe recalcitrants emphasizes these parallels all the more. Their origins clearly deserve more scrutiny.

[42] On this family, see D. B. Zema "The Houses of Tuscany and of Pierleone in the Crisis of Rome in the Eleventh Century," *Traditio* 2 (1944): 155–75; and Stanley Chodorow, *Christian Political Theory and Church Politics in the Mid-Twelfth Century* (Berkeley, 1972), 31 ff.; and see my essay in *Studies in the History of the Jewish People and the Land of Israel* 5 (1980): 75–90, for a detailed discussion of the Pierleoni and the Jews. There the origin of the *Sicut Iudaeis* bull is discussed at length.

[43] For Benzo, *MGH*, Scriptores XI, 616; and cf. the modern echo of this in, e.g., Walter Ullmann, *A Short History of the Papacy in the Middle Ages* (London, 1977), p. 175.

[44] See the texts of Arnulf, Manfred, and Bernard cited in David Berger, "The Attitude of St. Bernard of Clairvaux Toward the Jews," *Proceedings of the American Academy for Jewish Research 40* (1972): 89–108; and see Chodorow, *Political Theory*, pp. 27–47 for a general summary of the struggle in the 1130s.

[45] Adolf Jellinek, *Bet Ha-Midrash*, 6: 137–39 and Moses Gaster, *The Ma^{c}aseh Book* (Phila., 1934), pp. 188, 412–14.

[46] On Pierleoni politics see Chodorow, *Political Theory*, pp. 30–31.

[47] On families, clients and patronage in general in the Middle Ages, see Jacques Heers, *Le clan familial au Moyen Age* (Paris, 1974), *passim*; on families in Rome, Robert Brentano, *Rome Before Avignon* (New York, 1974), esp. chap. 5; and with reference to the Pierleoni, Tillman Schmidt, *Alexander II und die Römische Reform Gruppe Seiner Zeit* (Stuttgart, 1977), 64; cf. Hermann Vogelstein and Paul Rieger, *Geschichte der Juden in Rom* (Berlin, 1895), 1: 218–19.

[48] See Baron, *SRH*, 4: 93–4 and 5: 199 and 284 n. 4; Ullmann, *Short History*, 142, and Gabriel Jackson, *The Making of Medieval Spain* (New York, 1972), 56.

[49] Bernardino Llorca, "Derechos de la Santa Sede sobre España. El pensamiento de Gregorio VII," *Sacerdozio e Regno*, pp. 79–106.

[50] Frederick Russell, *The Just War in the Middle Ages*, (Cambridge, 1978), p. 110 ff.

[51] On these disputes, see P. Duchesne, *The Beginnings of the Temporal Authority of the Popes*, trans. A. M. Matthew (New York, 1972 of 1908 orig.), 268 and Benzo of Alba, *MGH*, *Scriptores (SS)* XI, 616; and Zema, "The Houses of Pierleone," p. 174.

[52] A previous contact of this sort, in 952, is discussed in Jacob Mann, *Texts and Studies*, pp. 14 f.

[53] See, e.g., Johannes Ramackers, *Papsturkunden in Frankreich*, (Berlin, 1932–33), vol. 2, No. 6, p. 30; vol. 3, no. 3, p. 34, and esp. no. 4, p. 36, and vol. 4, no. 8, p. 72.

[54] Cited in Philip Jaffe, *Monumenta Gregoriana* (Berlin, 1865), p. 472.

[55] See Browe, *Judenmission*, p. 235; Grayzel in "The Bull, Sicut," 244; and Georg Caro, *Sozial- und Wirtschaftsgeschichte der Juden in Mittelalter und der Neuzeit* (1908–18), 1: 288 and 496. Baron *SRH*, 4: 7 and 236, n. 4 opposes this view, and sees the text as a response to a petition of Roman Jews fearful of the results expected from the 1123 Lateran Council.

[56] PL 161: 820, *Decretum*, Part XIII, paragraphs 101 and 105, letters of Gregory I, and paragraphs 114 and 115, letters of Alexander II. Cf. too the citation of Gregory in Burchard of Worms, PL 140: 742, *Decretorum Libri XX*, 4, par. 91 and in Gratian *Decretum*, esp. D. 45, c. 3, and, there, C. 23, q. 8, c. 11, for the text of Alexander II.

[57] Norman Golb, "New Light on The Persecution of French Jews at the Time of the

First Crusade," *PAAJR* 34 (1966): 1–64, and *History and Culture of the Jews of Rouen in the Middle Ages* (in Hebrew), (Tel Aviv, 1976), chap. 3, argues vigorously that the Rouen attack took place. But see Hans Liebeschutz, "The Crusading Movement and Its Bearing on the Christian Attitudes Towards Jewry," *Journal of Jewish Studies* 10 (1959): 97–111, pointing to the impact of the episcopally directed peace-movement on preventing assaults, and esp. p. 107, asserting that the French were indeed following the lead of Alexander II. On Urban II and the peace movement see Jules Gay, *Les Papes du XIe Siècle* (reprint, New York, 1972), pp. 374–82, and esp. 374–75.

[58] See Ms. Oxford-Bodleian 847, fol. 36, a copy of which is available in The Microfilm Institute of the Hebrew University and National Library, Jerusalem, No. 21608. I wish to thank Dr. Abraham David for sharing his knowledge of this chronicle with me.

[59] Wibert's Letter in Aronius, *Regesten*, p. 94. On Wibert as the recognized Pope in Germany, Albert Hauck, in *Real Encyklopaedie für Protestantische Theologie und Kirche* (reprint, Graz, 1971), 21: 218. For the problems of Henry IV, fighting in Italy, see Zema, "The House of Pierleone," p. 170, and for his maneuvering with the German bishops, see Sara Schiffmann, "Heinrichs IV Verhalten zu den Juden zur Zeit des ersten Kreuzzuges," and "Die Deutschen Bischöfe und die Juden zur Zeit des Ersten Kreuzzuges," *Zeitschrift für die Geschichte der Juden in Deutschland* 3 (1931): 39 and 233.

[60] As did Cecil Roth in the *Encyclopeadia Judaica* (Jerusalem, 1971), s.v. "Popes."

[61] D. Berger, "Bernard," *PAAJR* 40 (1972): 90–92.

[62] See Baron, *SRH*, 4: 7, and Grayzel, "Sicut," 245.

[63] See Chodorow, *Political Theory*, pp. 27–47.

[64] Bernard's statement is in PL 182: 567; Humbert's in J. D. Mansi, *Sacrorum Conciliorum Collectio* (Venice, 1779–82), 59 vols., 24: 115. On Bernard and Jewish lending, my forthcoming, "The Church and Neutral Historiography." *Jewish Historiography and World History* (Mercaz Shazar, Jerusalem).

[65] Baldus (d. 1400), *Consilia* (1575), 5: no. 428. For the canons, see Emil Friedberg, ed., *Corpus Iuris Canonicis* (Leipzig, 1879–1881), 2 vols; Marquardus de Susannis, *De Iudaeis et Aliis Infidelibus* (Venice, 1558). See also the briefer, yet rounded theological discussions in Raymond Penaforte, *Summa de Poenitentia et Matrimonio* (Rome, 1603), and Alexander of Hales, *Summa Theologica* (Quaracchi, 1924–1928), 4 vols.

[66] In this year, Pius V expelled Jews from the Papal State, specifically for violating the terms of *Sicut Iudaeis* irreparably; see K. R. Stow, *Catholic Thought and Papal Jewry Policy*, pp. 34–37.

[67] See James Parkes, *The Conflict of The Church and The Synagogue* (reprint, Phila., 1961), Appendix One; and Blumenkranz, *Juifs et Chrétiens*, pp. 291–372 for synopses and surveys of such legislation in the years 300–1100.

[68] Composed originally around 953, ed. "Hominer" (Jerusalem, 1968), ch. 77, p. 291: "The head of all the bishops in the world in governance (jurisdiction)—the bishop of Rome . . ." (my translation, as is the case with all subsequent translations of Hebrew texts); and see David Flusser, ed., *Sefer Yossipon*, 2 vols. (Jerusalem, 1978–79), 2: 33–34.

[69] "Vikuaḥ R. Yaᶜacov Mivinişya," ed. J. Kabak, in *Ginze Nistarot* (Bamberg, 1868), 1: 29–30 and J. B. Eisenstein, *ᶜOṣar Vikuḥim* (New York, 1929), p. 192: "The King above all the kings . . ." Although not always up to high standards of textual editing, Eisenstein will be cited because of its accessibility; and see Joseph Shatzmiller "Did Nicholas Donin Promulgate the Blood Libel," *Studies in the History of the Jewish People and the Land of Israel* 4 (1978): 181–82. On the identity of Jacob b. Elie, see K. R. Stow, "Jacob b. Elie and Jewish Settlement in Venice," *Italia* 4 (1985).

[70] L. Finkelstein, *Jewish Self-Government in the Middle Ages* (reprint, New York,

1964), pp. 328 and 337, par. 1.

[71] *Seder Eliyahu Zuta*, ed. Shelomo Simonsohn and Meir Benayahu (Jerusalem, 1977), 2: 259 and 260.

[72] *Milḥemet Miṣvah*, ms. Parma, 2749, fols. 42^{v} and 125$^{r \& v}$; and see also fol. 228^{v} where Meir says, "You say the pope has as much power as that *man* in the heavens," i.e. The pope is Vicarius Christi. See too n. 96 below.

[73] See this in detail in Marc Saperstein, *Decoding the Rabbis* (Cambridge, Mass., 1980), pp. 103–6.

[74] Eisenstein, *Oṣar*, "Vikuaḥ Ha-Ramban" pp. 88 and 90, and H. D. Chavel, ed., *Kitve Ha-Ramban* (Jerusalem, 1963), vol. 1, pp. 306 and 312.

[75] Ernst Benz, *Ecclesia Spiritualis* (Stuttgart, 1934), Part III, chaps. 3 and esp. 4, part 3, and cf. Yitzhak Baer "The Historical Background of the Raya Mehemna," *Zion* 5 (1940): 1–44.

[76] Simeon b. Ṣemah Duran, in Eisenstein, ᶜ*Oṣar*, "Vikuaḥ Ha- Rashbaṣ," p. 126.

[77] On Benedict XIII, see Stow, *Catholic Thought*, pp. 278–89.

[78] On this title and its meaning, see most recently Stephan Kuttner, "Universal Pope or Servant of God's Servants: the Canonists, Papal Titles and Innocent III," *Revue de droit canonique* 32 (1981): 109–49.

[79] Composed by Josef b. Natan Official, ed. Judah Rosenthal (Jerusalem, 1970), pp. 86 and 105.

[80] Ed. J. Ch. Wagenseil in *Tela Ignea Satanae* (Frankfurt a.m., 1861), col. 250.

[81] "Sefer Klimat ha-Goyim," Eisenstein, ᵓ*Oṣar*, pp. 279–80, and ed. N. Posnanski in *Ha-Ṣofeh Me-ᵓereṣ Hagar* 3 (1913), 99 f., 143 f. and 4 (1914): 37, 81, 115 and esp. 41–42. See also Frank Talmage, ed., *The Polemical Writings of Profiat Duran* (in Hebrew) (Jerusalem, 1981), pp. 30, 35, 44, 45, 81, as well as the introductory comments on pp. 16–21 (Hebrew pagination).

[82] "Bitul ᶜIqarei Dat Ha-Noṣrim," Eisenstein, *Oṣar*, pp. 307–30, and ed. E. Deinard (Kearny, N.J., 1904), pp. 62–63.

[83] *Sefer Ha-ᶜIqqarim/Book of Principles*, Maᵓamar 3, chap. 25, ed. I. Husik (Phila., 1946), 3: 241, Eisenstein, *Oṣar*, "Vikuaḥ R. Yosef Albo," pp. 114–15.

[84] de Susannis, *de Iudaeis*, Part I, chap. 11, par. 13; Michael Wilks, *The Problem of Sovereignty in the Later Middle Ages* (Cambridge, 1963), pp. 316 and 467; and S. Hendrix, "In Quest of the *Vera Ecclesia*: The Crises of Late Medieval Ecclesiology," *Viator* 7 (1976): 362.

[85] "Klimat ha-Goyim," Eisenstein, *Oṣar*, p. 280 and Posnanski, p. 100; and "Bitul ᶜIqarei Dat ha-Noṣrim," Eisenstein, p. 307, and Deinard, p. 62.

[86] Ed. Shemuel Greenbaum (Thorn, 1873), pp. 2 and 12; and Eisenstein, *Oṣar*, pp. 82 and 86.

[87] "Vikuaḥ R. Yaᶜacov," Eisenstein, *Oṣar*, p. 192 and Kabak, p. 29; and see Grayzel *XIIIth Century*, p. 340, for the debate on the identity of the King in this tract. Shatzmiller, however, "Nicolas Donin," p. 181, is correct in seeing the reference is to the pope.

[88] Ed. J. Rosenthal, *Meḥqarim u-Meqorot*, 2 vols. (Jerusalem, 1967), 1: 420, where the author writes of a letter sent to the King of France by the pope defending the right of French Jews to protection.

[89] Ed. A. Shohat (Jerusalem, 1956), chaps. 14 and 41. There the pope is called *Ḥasid* and *Ohev Yehudim*. Ibn Verga normally reserved these terms for favored kings who saved the Jews, or at least made serious efforts at doing so. On this see Yerushalmi, *Lisbon Massacre*, pp. 42 and 49.

[90] Ed. Wagenseil, col. 259: "The heretics (converts) say: The Talmud twists and

perverts all of our Torah and keeps us from understanding the essence and the truth;" cf. Grayzel, *XIIIth Century*, p. 240, no. 96 where Gregory IX (June 9, 1239) states: "lege veteri . . . non contenti . . . affirmant legem aliam . . . Talmut . . . Cum igitur hec dicitur esse causa precipua, que Judeos in sua tenet perfidia obstinatos, . . ." The "dicitur" refers, of course, to Nicholas Donin, as Gregory himself indicates (Grayzel, no. 95).

[91] Grayzel, *ibid.*, e.g. p. 226 (pogroms), pp. 262–66 (blood libels), p. 268 (interest), p. 274 (Talmud). For an explicit, although later, response to a Jewish request on sermons, see the letter of Martin V (20 Feb. 1422), in Moritz Stern, *Urkundliche Beitraege ueber die Stellung der Paepste zu den Juden*, no. 21; for the 13th century, see Stow, *Catholic Thought*, p. 20, no. 59 and see J. M. Vidal, *Bullaire de l'inquisition française au XIV*^{e} *siècle* (Paris, 1913), nn. 269–70, for a bull of restraint by Boniface VIII.

[92] For papal agreement to forced preaching, see Browe, *Judenmission*, pp. 13–55; on the Talmud, Grayzel, nn. 95–98 and Browe, p. 75; on the inquisition, the bull, *Turbato Corde*, in *Bullarium . . . Romanum* (Turin, 1858), 3: 796, Browe, pp. 252–66 and, Joseph Shatzmiller, "L'inquisition et les juifs de Provence au XIIe siècle," *Provence Historique* 23 (1973): 327–38, where, incidentally, it is seen that individuals were occasionally acquitted by inquisitional courts.

[93] Browe, *ibid.*, p. 76, n. 69.

[94] For the censure by Innocent III of the anti-usury activities of Robert Courson, see J. W. Baldwin, *Masters, Princes and Merchants*, 2 vols. (Princeton, 1970), 1: 297; and see below on the resistance of Odo of Chateauroux to Innocent IV on the Talmud question.

[95] See e.g., the references, cited in n. 91 above to Grayzel, Vidal and Stern; and see also Finkelstein, *Jewish Self-Government*, 281 and 337.

[96] Ms. Parma 2749, for which no edition exists. See Siegfried Stein, *Jewish Christian Disputations in Thirteenth Century Narbonne* (London, 1969) and R. Chazan's articles on aspects of the *Milḥemet Miṣvah* along with copious translations from the text, in *PAAJR*, 41–42 (1973–74): 45–67, *Hebrew Union College Annual* 45 (1974): 287–305, and *Harvard Theological Review* 67 (1974): 437–57.

[97] *Milḥemet Miṣvah* (hence *M.M.*), fols. 64^{R}–83^{R}.

[98] M.M. 17^{R}–37^{V}; esp. 32^{R}; 60^{V}–61^{R}; and 214^{R}–218^{V}.

[99] M.M. 32^{R}, 70^{V} and 214^{V}; on Louis IX on usury, see Chazan, *Medieval Jewry*, pp. 110–21; and on the whole problem of popes, kings and usury, see K. R. Stow, "Papal and Royal Attitudes Toward Jewish Lending in the Thirteenth Century," *AJS Review* 6 (1981): 161–84.

[100] M.M. 71^{R}.

[101] Grayzel, *XIIIth Century*, p. 200 (n. 70) and cf. p. 268 (n. 15), the text of Innocent IV.

[102] M.M. 33^{V} and 228^{V}.

[103] M.M. $1^{R\,\&\,V}$ and 214^{R}–220^{V}.

[104] M.M. 71^{V}, and cf. 65^{R}, 68^{R}, 70^{V}, and 226^{V}.

[105] M.M. 32^{R}, 33^{V}, and 214^{V}.

[106] M.M. 70^{V}–71^{R}, cf. Chazan in *HUCA* 45 (1974): 300.

[107] M.M. 42^{V}; cf. 33^{V} and 125^{R}.

[108] R. W. and A. J. Carlyle, *A History of Medieval Political Theory in the West* (New York, 1936), 3rd impression, is still an excellent introduction to these questions. More technical, and valuable for its critique of W. Ullmann's *Medieval Papalism* is A. M. Stickler's "Concerning the Political Theories of The Medieval Canonists," *Traditio* 7 (1949–51): 450–63.

[109] See especially the references to the canonists Johannes Teutonicus (p. 298) and Huguccio (p. 301) in Gaines Post "Two Notes on Nationalism."

[110] Ms. Parma, de Rossi 563, ed. in Haberman, *Sefer Gezerot*, pp. 19–21 and most recently by Norman Golb, *The Jews of Rouen*, pp. 71–73 (see the facsimile of the MS in the Appendix below); and cf. Robert Chazan, "1007–1012, Initial Crisis for Northern European Jewry," *PAAJR* 39 (1972): 101–18.

[111] See Blumenkranz, *Juifs et Chrétiens*, p. 136 and Golb, *Rouen*, pp. 13 f., who gives a full identification of characters; Chazan, "Initial Crisis," *passim*; S. Schwarzfuchs, "Jacob bar Yekoutièl chez le Pape" (essentially a French trans. of the original). *Evidences*, 6, no. 41 (1954): 36–37; Vogelstein-Rieger, *Juden in Rom*, 1: 212 and Baron, *SRH*, 4: 57 and 265, n. 74, who does, however, call the incident "obscure" and "alleged."

[112] I. Levi, "Les Juifs de France du milieu du IXe siècle aux croisades," *REJ*, 52 (1906): 161–68.

[113] *MGH, SS*. III, 81 (and see Blumenkranz, *Auteurs*, p. 250).

[114] On this, see Graetz, *Geschichte der Juden*, 5: 387 and 545 and cf. n. 125 below.

[115] *PL*. 142: 657 (and see Blumenkranz, *Auteurs*, 256).

[116] Baron, *SRH*, 4: 57, followed by Chazan, "Initial Crisis," tries to weave the acts of *Al-Hakim*, the reports of the Christian chronicles and 1007 together. With respect to Glaber's claim about "the common will," 1007 does speak of the "Peoples of the World" plotting against the Jews. Nevertheless, 1007 continues straight off by discussing those whom it identifies as the real movers of the attack, the king and the barons. Whence, the reference to the "Peoples . . ." should probably be read together with 1007's general references to "enemies" (unspecified) who carry out the attack; i.e., mob violence *following* that of the king. So too, this reference should be linked to those concerning Jewish suicide, a subject 1007 discusses in terms reminiscent of the language of the twelfth century Jewish Crusade chronicles.

[117] *MGH, SS*., *IV*, 136 (and see Blumenkranz, *Auteurs*, p. 250). Glaber also reports the tale of Raynaud of Sens, the allegedly judaizing count whom Robert the Pious unquestionably did attack. (*PL* 142: 657). Hence, it seems strange that Glaber neither reported the persecution of 1007 outright, nor linked it in some way to the Raynaud episode, assuming, of course, that there actually was a persecution in 1007 for Glaber to report. On Glaber's untrustworthiness in general, see David Herlihy, "The Agrarian Revolution in France and Italy; 801–1150," in *The Social History of Italy and Western Europe 700–1500* (London, 1978), p. 31.

[118] *MGH, SS*, *IV*, 139, and see too *ibid*, 136 for the incident in Limoges in 1010. Bishop Audouin forced the Jews to convert or leave Limoges. Three or four Jews converted; the rest left the city. (Blumenkranz, *Auteurs*, p. 250). Here again, no king is involved.

[119] The popes of the period were: John XVIII (1004–1009); Sergius IV (1009–1012); and Benedict VIII (1012–1024). Jacob spent at least four full years in Rome with no apparent change in pope. Clearly, this creates either a chronological problem, or a problem with Ademar's credibility. Cf. Chazan, "Initial Crisis," p. 107, n. 16, and Blumenkranz, *Juifs et Chrétiens*, p. 136.

[120] See the texts in translation, along with comments and bibliography in Walter Wakefield and Austin Evans, *Heresies of the High Middle Ages*, (New York, 1969), pp. 79–91; and the important notes of Ch. Pfister, *Études sur le regne de Robert le Pieux (996–1031)*, (Paris, 1885), pp. 331–38, especially with relation to the Jews and burning as a punishment, applied here for the first time against heretics.

[121] See, e.g. Blumenkranz, *Auteurs*, pp. 73–74, 142–44 and 174; and cf. Luther's charge of Judaizing (through observing the Sabbath), which he linked to direct Jewish influence. *Against the Sabbatarians* in *Luther's Works*, ed. and trans. M. Bertram, (Phila., 1971), 47: 59–98.

[122] Edward I, cited in Thomas Rymer, *Foedera* (London, 1816), I, 1, 539, text of Dec. 13, 1276, also cited in Emil Friedberg, *De finium inter ecclesiam et civitatem regundorum judicio* (Leipzig, 1965 reprint of 1861), p. 103.

[123] Most notably, Helgaud de Fleury in *Vie de Robert le Pieux*, ed. and trans., R. H. Bautier and G. Labory (Paris, 1965), who stresses Robert's piety and pious works.

[124] Pfister, *Robert le Pieux*, pp. 31–32, records that despite the existence of a diploma of Robert The Pious, dated 1022, Glaber, in his history, wrote, "tertio de vicesimo . . . anno," i.e., 1017 (easily rectified to 1022—depending on the calendar in use—by amending "et" for "de"). Thus 1017 became the accepted date for the Orleans heresy, even in Caesar Baronius *Annales Ecclesiastici* (Lucca, 1744), 16: 507–8, where perhaps by sheer coincidence the story of Benedict VIII's burning of Jews follows immediately the Orleans story. Compounding the error, 1017 in Hebrew letters = תשע"ז, could easily have been miscopied into תשס"ז = 1007. And thus it occurred even written out fully in words in the unique extant ms. which dates from the 14th century. There is, in fact, no reason to accept or justify the date 1007, apart from the ms.; and cf. Chazan and Blumenkranz in n. 119 above, who both reject 1007 as a precise date.

[125] Graetz, *Geschichte*, 5: 544, points to problems in Germany. His evidence is properly doubted by H. Tykocinski in *Festschrift M. Philippsons* (Leipzig, 1916), pp. 1–5, especially that furnished by a dirge ascribed third hand to R. Gershon of Mainz (ed. Haberman, *Gezerot*, pp. 16–18); still, the dirge does indicate instances of forced conversion in the early eleventh century, whoever the instigators may have been.

[126] George Duby ed., *L'An Mil* (Paris, 1967), pp. 33–36.

[127] Haberman, *Gezerot*, pp. 19 and 25–26; the term "Yirat Ha-Shem," particularly associated with the 12th and 13th century Hasidei Ashkenaz, also appears.

[128] See Paul Bonenfant, "Du Duché de Basse Lotharingie au Duché de Brabant," *Revue belge de philologie et d'histoire* 46 (1968): 1129–65, esp. 1130 and 1164–65; and L. Genicot, *Études sur les principautes Lotharingiennes* (Louvain, 1965), pp. 1–11 and esp. p. 1, and *The Encyclopedia Britannica*, eleventh ed. s.v. "Lorraine."

[129] The letter appears in S. D. Luzzatto, *Bet Ha-Oṣar* (Lvov, 1881), pp. 104–08.

[130] See Louis Finkelstein, *Jewish Self Government in the Middle Ages* (New York, 1924) p. 153, where Lothair is synonymous with Champagne, at the least, and p. 159, especially, where Jewish settlement is divided between Tsarfat, Lothair and Ashkenaz, making of Lothair almost a catch-all term.

[131] Jean Stengers, *Les Juifs dans les Pays Bas au Moyen Age* (Brussells, 1950), pp. 85–86, and cf. the similar opinion of J. Aronius in his *Regesten* no. 699, where he voices his suspicions about the claim made by an 18th century chronicle that an expulsion of Jews from Flanders occurred ca. 1120; but cf. Baron, *SRH*, 4: 265, n. 4, for his out of hand dismissal of Stengers.

[132] On papal chancery income, see W. E. Lunt, *Papal Revenues in the Middle Ages* (New York, 1934), 1: 125–29, and 2: 499, where a fee as high as 128 pounds is listed for a single bull.

[133] On Blois, see Haberman, *Gezerot*, pp. 124–25; note, too, the 60,000 pounds paid in the Bristol tallage of 1210 to King John of England, and see R. W. Emery, *The Jews of Perpignan* (New York, 1959), pp. 18, 30, & 130 for Jewish loans and prices in the 13th

century. Two hundred pounds would have purchased eight horses of average to respectable quality and, thus, was certainly insufficient to redeem the bulk of Northern French Jewry. On papal income in the hundreds of thousands, by way of contrast, see J. H. Mundy, *Europe in the High Middle Ages* (New York, 1973), pp. 324–25, 335–37, and 351–52. As for the fee offered the bishop, see the 13th century monetary conversion table in Eshtori haParḥi, *Kaftor va-Peraḥ* (Jerusalem, 1899), pp. 411–15.

[134] See Leopold Delisle, "Des Revenus Publics en Normandie au Douzième Siècle," *Bibliothèque de l'École des Chartres* 10 (1848–49): 178–210, especially 183; P. Guilhiermoz, "Note sur les poids du moyen-âge," *ibid.* 67 (1906): 200; and Etienne Fournial, *Histoire Monétaire de l'Occident Médiéval* (Paris, 1970), pp. 78–96, 161–82, and esp. 174.

[135] J. F. Lemarignier, *Le Gouvernment Royal aux premiers temps capétiens (987–1108)*, (Paris, 1965), p. 59; and Lemarignier, "Les Institutions Ecclésiastiques en France de la fin du Xe siècle," in Vol. III, Ferdinand Lot et Robert Fawtier, eds., *Histoire des Institutions Françaises au Moyen Age*, (Paris, 1962), pp. 42–49.

[136] C. W. Hollister and J. W. Baldwin, "The Rise of Administrative Kingship: Henry I and Philip Augustus," *American Historical Review*, 83 (1978): 902–04. See further, Joseph Strayer, "The Laicization of French and English Society in the XIIIth Century," *Speculum* 15 (1940): 76–86. The argument here is not that prelates were never close royal advisors after the twelfth century. Rather, from this time, the emphasis was placed increasingly on lay councillors. The terminology of 1007 is, moreover, that normally used for laymen.

[137] Haberman, *Gezerot*, 19. The Hebrew, "Sarai Va-Avadai," means officials and ministers, not ecclesiastics. The Esther theme is pervasive. Jacob b. Yekutiel is in many ways a latter day Mordechai, and the papal emissary who goes from place to place armed with a bull ordering an end to the persecution recalls the letter of Ahashuerus foiling Haman's plot (without, of course, the vengeance of the real Purim).

[138] See Y. Congar, *L'Ecclésiologie du Haut Moyen Age* (Paris, 1968), p. 64, on the concept of *Populus Dei* in the Carolingian Period; and W. Ullmann, *The Carolingian Renaissance* (London, 1969), *passim*, for the overall social and political ramifications of this concept in the 9th century.

[139] See Joseph Strayer, "France: The Holy Land, The Chosen People and The Most Christian King," in *Medieval Statecraft and the Perspectives of History* (Princeton, 1971), pp. 300–315. On the "spiritual" aspects of early nation-states see Gabriel Le Bras, *Institutions Ecclesiastiques de la chrétienté médiévale* (Paris, 1964), pp. 565–96; Georges de Lagarde, *La naissance de l'esprit laique au declin du moyen age*, 5 vols., 3rd ed. (Paris, 1956), 1: 183–88; and E. H. Kantorowicz, *The King's Two Bodies* (Princeton, 1957), chap. 5, *passim*. Kantorowicz, on another occasion, "Kingship and Scientific Jurisprudence," in *Twelfth Century Europe and The Foundations of Modern Society*, ed. Marshal Clagett et al. (Madison, 1961), p. 101, summed up the processes referred to here most pointedly: "What happened then was not a secularization of the spiritual, but rather a spiritualization and sanctification of the secular." It should be stressed here that this process is to be distinguished from the claim kings had made before the Gregorian Reform to be the heads of the Church(es) in their domains. Nor is it to be confused with the concept of sacral kingship. See Morrison, *The Two Kingdoms* and the earlier literature cited there on those problems, and G. Ladner as cited in n. 38 above.

[140] Gaines Post in "Two Notes on Nationalism," pp. 290–95.

[141] It has been argued that the permission to act given the inquisition by Philip IV, or its revocation, stood in direct correlation with the state of Philip's relations with the

papacy, and Boniface VIII in particular; see, e.g. Solomon Grayzel, "Popes, Jews and Inquisition—from '*Sicut*' to '*Turbato*'" in *Essays on the Occasion of the Seventieth Anniversary of the Dropsie University* (Philadelphia, 1979), pp. 151–88. However, the problem was really jurisdictional. Philip IV did not dispute the correctness of prosecuting Jews for the charges leveled by the Inquisition; see Gustave Saige, *Les Juifs du Languedoc* (Paris, 1881), pp. 232–34. He, however, did question whether the Inquisition should act against Jews without explicit royal sanction. The notion of direct Church jurisdiction over Jews was novel in Philip's day, see here below, and no king could have been expected to relinquish his exclusive powers over "Judaei nostri" without some well-defined and formal procedure; moreover, there was a definite movement of kings to usurp the powers of the Church outright. This went hand in hand with the drive of the kingdoms to become independent of the Church and to assume some of its spiritual authority and aura. On this, see Malcolm Barber, "The World Picture of Philip The Fair," *Journal of Medieval History* 8 (1982): 13–27.

[142] See *PL* 182: 567 for Bernard: "Peius iudaizare dolemus Christianos feneratores, si tamen Christianos, et non magis baptizatos Judaeos." On Bruges, Raymond de Roover *Money, Banking and Credit in Mediaeval Bruges* (Cambridge, Mass., 1948), p. 152.

[143] On the problem of royalty and the Talmud, see here below, and also the comments of Grayzel in "Popes, Jews, and Inquisition," *passim*. Roman Law, basically an academic concern (outside Italy), was nevertheless cited as precedent in court. Three texts may have influenced kings in particular: C.T. 16, 8, 18, the prototype of *Sicut iudaeis*, (see here above); C.J., Nov. 146, where Justinian asserted the right of the state to control Jewish literature in specifically religious matters; but, most of all, C.J. 1, 9, 8, which insists on state jurisdiction over Jews in questions "both civil and religious." In addition, the C.J. restricts Jews in much the same way as do the canons (whence, it was cited by canonists freely and frequently). In the increasingly spiritualized politics of the thirteenth century, these legal texts likely assumed a real and contemporary meaning. Indeed, this last text was that specifically cited by Johannes Teutonicus to indicate Jews were under Imperial rule; see G. Post, "Two Notes," p. 298, and cf. note 109 above.

[144] Romans 11:28.

[145] *MGH Epist. Karol Aevi* III, epist. 6, p. 181, 1.42 for *impedimentum*; on the idea of a pure society, see Gerhard Ladner, *The Idea of Reform* (Cambridge, Mass., 1959). For further descriptions of a society that had fully integrated Christian ideals into its consciousness and structures, see Marvin Becker, *Medieval Italy: Constraints and Creativity* (Bloomington, Indiana, 1981), pp. 19–58; and on medieval spirituality in general, see Andre Vauchez, *La spiritualite du Moyen Age occidental VIIIe–XIIe siècles* (Paris, 1975), pp. 75–145.

[146] Haberman, *Gezerot* 19. This same sentiment clearly lurks behind the 16th century comment of Yosef ha-Cohen in his ^c*Emek ha-Bakha*, ed. M. Letteris (Cracow, 1895), p. 71. Philip IV is credited by Joseph ha-Cohen with the following declaration when he expelled the Jews from France. "Every Jew must leave *my* land, taking none of his possessions with him; or, let him choose a new God for himself, and we will become *One People*." The accuracy of this attribution is a matter of some interest.

[147] See Kantorowicz, *KTB*, p. 251 on this phrase; and see also Gabrielle M. Speigel, "'Defence of the Realm': Evolution of a Capetian Propaganda Slogan," in *Journal of Medieval History* 3 (1977): 115–33, on the use of this concept in the chronicle tradition of St. Denis. The concept, evolving from the older idea of *tuitio*, was to be taken at face value, but also could be used as a tool of practical politics. On further propaganda efforts in chronicles, see Sophia Menache, "Vers une conscience nationale: Mythe et symbolisme

au début de la Guerre de Cent Ans," *Le Moyen Age*, 89 (1983): 85–97.

[148] On royal piety and its role in the establishment of Jewry policy, see Gavin Langmuir, "The Jews and the Archives of Angevin England," *Traditio* 19 (1963): 183–244, "Judaei Nostri," *Traditio* 16 (1960): 203–69 and Langmuir's review of B. Bachrach's *Early Medieval Jewish Policy* in *Speculum* 54 (1979): 104; See too Wm. C. Jordan, *Louis IX and the Challenge of the Crusade: A Study in Rulership* (Princeton, 1979), p. 105 on the "intertwining" of the "emotional, the practical, and the spiritual" in the attitudes of Louis IX, and pp. 210–13 on Louis' use of the motto: *Christus Vincit, Christus Regnat, Christus Imperat*.

[149] See Samuel Krauss, "Apiphior, nom Hebreu du Pape," *REJ* 34 (1897): 235–38, together with the stricture of Carmoly in *Oṣar Neḥmad* 3 (1860): 110.

[150] Haberman, *Gezerot*, 20. The central phrase in this passage is *Memshelet Reshut*. The Jews are said to live *Be-Memshelet Reshutkhah*, v. lit. - governance of your sanction. This figure exists nowhere else in Hebrew literature and probably corresponds to the Latin *ius iudicandi, potestas iudicandi*, or *potestas iurisdictionis*, with *Memshalah* [governance] = power/right and *Reshut* [sanction] = court sanction. It should be noted that despite the absence of a textual reference in traditional literature for *Memshelet Reshut*, 1007 may have been playing on the oft-repeated *Memshelet Zadon* (the evil government). Jews prayed, as Christians complained—thinking (correctly?) the reference was to them— for an end to *Memshelet Zadon* (e.g., Additional Service, New Year; and see too J. Rosenthal in *JQR* 47 [1951], p. 62, par. 34). Hence 1007 was comparing, tacitly, the *Memshelet Reshut* (good, proper government) of the Pope to the *Memshelet Zadon* of the King. I thank the late Rabbi A. Chiel of Woodbridge, Conn., for this idea. See also below on Ehud ben Gerah.

[151] The best discussion of these issues appears in the writings of A. M. Stickler in *Traditio* 7 (1951) and *Sacerdozio e Regno*, noted above, esp. in their evaluation of the work of W. Ullmann. See too G. Catalano, *Impero, Regno e Sacerdozio nel Pensiero di Uguccio da Pisa* (Milano, 1959), esp. p. 43, for Huguccio on the right of the Pope to judge the Emperor and Kings; and Michael Wilks, *The Problem of Sovereignty, passim*, for maximalist theories of Papal Monarchism. Earlier statements, as those of Regino of Prum (915), Gregory VII, Anselm of Lucca (1083), and Manengold of Lautenbach (1103), tend toward monarchism (see Giovanni Pilati, *Chiesa e Stato nei primi quindici secoli* [Rome, 1961], pp. 115, 125, 157, 160–61, 162 and 165), occasionally using bombastic rhetoric, but certainly do not give the Pope direct jurisdiction in all matters, as does Alanus (Pilati, p. 213) and, to be sure, 1007. In fact, 1007, does not distinguish at all between spiritual and secular spheres of jurisdiction. The Jews are simply under the governance and jurisdiction of the Pope; and 1007 obviously knew how to divide fact from theory. He needed no one to tell him that the Jews were in reality the Chamber Serfs, etc., of the kings.

[152] See the Diss. of W. Pakter, *De His Qui Foris Sunt: The Teachings of the Medieval Canon and Civil Lawyers Concerning the Jews*, Johns Hopkins University (Baltimore, 1974), chap. 1, for a study of ecclesiastical claims to direct jurisdiction over Jews and their development. It was only with Innocent IV and Hostiensis that the claim of direct jurisdiction was made; and see, *ibid.*, p. 343, n. 85 for the commentary of Innocent IV on X, 3, 34, 8: *Quod super his*. But see now the full correct text and interpretation of B. Z. Kedar in "Canon Law and the Burning of the Talmud," *Bulletin of Medieval Canon Law* 9 (1979): 79–82. The pope, says Kedar, was insisting on the right to supervise the *purity of Judaism* when he claimed direct jurisdiction over certain Jewish matters. See also Joel Rembaum, "The Talmud and the Popes: Reflections on the Talmud Trials of the 1240s," *Viator* 13 (1982): 203–23.

[153] See especially Michele Maccarrone, "'Potestas directa' e 'Potestas indirecta' nei teologi del XII e XIII secolo," *Sacerdozio e Regno*, pp. 27–49.

[154] See Lemarignier, in Lot and Fawtier, *Histoire des Institutions*, 3: 47, for the decree of the 991 council of Chelles, and *ibid.*, pp. 42–47 and 55–62, for the king as a quasi-bishop, with episcopal support, and the episcopal uproar over papally granted monastic exemptions; on this see also Lemarignier, *Gouvernement Royal*, pp. 59 and 76, for further detail. Richard II of Normandy (*Institutions* 3: 60–62) was strong enough to insist that papal exemptions for monasteries pass directly through his hands. He obviously could have stopped a legate sent on a matter concerning Jews. Cf. Blumenkranz *Juifs et Chrétiens*, p. 136, n. 252, who notes that John XVIII sent a legate to France; but there is no indication that his mission dealt with Jews. Pfister, *Études*, pp. 51–60, concludes that Robert the Pious repudiated his wife Bertha because she was childless and not in defeat after five years of papal pressure. Finally, Raymonde Foreville, "The Synods of the Province of Rouen in Eleventh and Twelfth Centuries" in *Essays Presented to C. R. Cheney*, ed., C. N. L. Brooke, et al. (Cambridge, 1976), pp. 23–24, comments that the dukes of the eleventh century used legates for their own purposes, especially to elect or depose bishops; and the legates always deferred to ducal wishes.

[155] Pakter, *De His*, pp. 7–8.

[156] Grayzel, *XIIIth Century*, pp. 132–33.

[157] Pakter, *ibid.*, pp. 16–23.

[158] *Summa Theologica*, II, II, 10, 9, reply to Obj. 2.

[159] See n. 150 above.

[160] On Valreas, see Grayzel, *XIIIth Century* nos. 113 and 114, pp. 262–67 and Jordan, *Louis IX*, p. 86.

[161] M.M. 33[V].

[162] Wm. Cornot (Cornotensis), O.P., and royal chaplain, relates this in Bouquet, *Recueil des Historiens des Gaules et de la France* (Paris, 1738–1865): 20:34, *De vita et Miraculis Sancti Ludovici.*

[163] *Ibid.*, and see the discussion of Gérard Nahon, "Le Crédit et les Juifs dans la France du XIIIe siècle," *Annales* 24 (1969): 1137–38, especially on the matter of the restitution of interest already collected. On the expulsion of usurers see Jordan, *Louis IX*, pp. 85, 86, 154–55.

[164] M.M. 71[R].

[165] See Cecil Roth, *A History of the Jews in England* (Oxford, 1949), pp. 65–69; and the texts in Saige, *Les Juifs du Languedoc antérieurement au XIVe siècle* (1971, reprint of 1881) pp. 227–28; E. J. de Laurière, *Ordonnances des rois de la troisième race*, 22 vols. (Paris, 1723–1849), 1: 545; and cf. Chazan, *Medieval Jewry*, pp. 228–29; and E. Scheid, "Catalogue des Documents du Trésor des Chartres" *REJ* 2 (1881): 31; so too Baron *SRH* 12: 138–69.

[166] Saige, p. 224.

[167] Saige, pp. 212–13 and 235–36.

[168] Roth, pp. 56 and 78.

[169] See Langmuir, "*Judaei Nostri*," and "The Archives," *passim.*

[170] For the expanded *Turbato Corde* text, see Saige, pp. 232–33, and for the original, see Browe, *Judenmission*, p. 258, also with notes on the reissues of the bull and the location of additional printed versions. And see Grayzel, *XIIIth Century*, pp. 262, 268 and 274, for papal rejection of blood libels.

[171] The problem is: After the fact, everyone took credit for the burnings; before, the outstanding points are (1) that all the papal correspondence, including the papal

letters to be forwarded to kings in other countries, was sent to Wm. of Auvergne and Odo of Chateauroux *in Paris*; (2) that the inquisitorial process and examination of books and rabbis took place *only at Paris*; and (3) that it was *only at Paris* that the Talmud was burned. The language of the letters, furthermore, shows that the popes neither initiated nor quite understood what was happening. The condemnation engineered by Odo in 1248 reveals his central role in the entire episode. The papal letters and other pertinent literature are to be found, along with discussion, in Grayzel, *XIIIth Century*, pp. 29–33, 238–45, 250–53 and 274–81; and in Ch. M. Merchavia, *The Church versus Talmudic and Midrashic Literature* (Jerusalem, 1970), pp. 227–45, and see p. 248 for the actual date of the burning.

[172] Cited in Grayzel, p. 274, in a letter to Louis IX, which, in turn, cites the no longer extant letter to Odo. It may have been that Innocent had come to share the position espoused by contemporary Spanish Dominicans who favored censorship, perhaps for the conversionary exploitation of Rabbinic Texts; on which see Grayzel, p. 33, n. 66; Baer, *Christian Spain* 2: 229; and Browe, *Judenmission*, pp. 75–79. A further bull of this nature was issued in 1258 by Alexander IV and sent to the rulers of Burgundy and Anjou (as well as to the king, although in the letter to him no mention was made of books, but only of the decrees of the Fourth Lateran Council, a subject also raised in the letters to Burgundy and Anjou). In these letters, Alexander IV specified only the confiscation and not the burning of Hebrew texts, apparently anticipating either expurgation or a selective procedure condemning only blasphemous material; see the text in I. Loeb, "Bulles inèdites des papes," *REJ* 1 (1880): 116–17. Subsequently, Clement IV explicitly indicated censorship in his letters of the 1260s to James I of Aragon; for which see Heinrich Denifle, "Quellen zur Disputation Pablos Christiani mit Mose Nachmani zu Barcelona, 1263," *Historisches Jahrbuch des Goerres Gesellschaft* 8 (1887): 225–44.

[173] See Amos Funkenstein, "Changes in the Patterns of Anti-Jewish Polemics in the 12th Century," (in Hebrew) *Zion* 33 (1968): 137–42. But note that from the time of the letters of Alexander IV (n. 172) and on, the Talmud was attacked only for its blasphemies. Cf. esp. the Inquisitional texts cited by Grayzel, *XIIIth Century*, App. B, pp. 341–43 (now correctly dated by Yerushalmi in *Harvard Theological Review* 63 (1970): 351, as 14th century writs). Perhaps the popes feared an attack on the extra-scriptural nature of Talmudic law might lead to a similar attack on extra-scriptural papal legislation (i.e., the body of the Decretals). Indeed, motives of this kind may already have been active in Paris in 1239, pitting the scripturally oriented theologians of the University against the curially slanted canonists and eventually the popes themselves. For reasons that are self-evident, however, no written mention of these motives was made.

[174] In Merchavia, *Ha-Talmud*, pp. 451–52, including the signatures; and see I. Loeb, "Bulles inèdites des papes," *REJ* 1 (1880): 294–95, who argues that Odo's condemnation produced no new confiscation or burning.

[175] See these letters in Grayzel, *XIIIth Century*, nos. 113, 114, 115, 116 and 117.

[176] For Louis IX's order, also accusing the Jews of magic and blasphemy, see Grayzel, *XIIIth Century*, p. 337, and Baron, *SRH*, 9: 67 and 271, n. 15.

[177] M.M. 33^{V}. See here, Jordan, *Louis IX*, pp. 23, 128–29, 182 and 205.

[178] See the reference to B. Z. Kedar in n. 152 above.

[179] On the consciousness of due process (of course, without the name), see J. A. Watt, "The Term 'Plenitudo Potestatis' in Hostiensis," *Proceedings of the Second International Congress of Medieval Canon Law*, ed. S. Kuttner (Vatican City, 1965), pp. 161–87, esp. p. 174.

[180] See here Malcolm Barber, "The World Picture of Philip The Fair," pp. 13–20.

[181] See Jacob Katz, *Exclusiveness and Tolerance* (New York, 1962), pp. 13–63, and

esp. p. 23 on Christianity and idolatry.

[182] A canon decree on this, although with certain minor circumlocutions, was issued by Boniface VIII in the sixth book of Decretals (Sext. 5, 2, 13). It made official what had been accepted practice. Cf. *Decretals* (X, 3, 42, 3) for a text of Innocent III on this subject, which does not discuss Jews directly; for a text that does, see Gratian *Decretum*, D. 45, c. 5, incorporating the famous decree of the 633 Fourth Toledan Council (Mansi, 10: 633) against backsliding. However, it seems that a consensus was achieved only in the 12th century, with Gratian. In 1096, it appears that Anti-pope Clement III sought to enforce the Toledan decree, while pope Urban II did not, following the practice of Gregory the Great. Cf. note 58 above.

[183] On the problems of the Jews with the Inquisition, see M. Kriegel, "Premarranisme et inquisition dans la Provence des XIIIe et XIVe siècles," *Provence Historique* 29 (1978): 313–23; and Y. H. Yerushalmi, "The Inquisition and the Jews of France in the Time of Bernard Gui," *Harvard Theological Review* 63 (1970): 317–76.

[184] See, e.g., Shatzmiller, "L'inquisition et les juifs de Provence," in *Provence Historique*, 1973, p. 332.

[185] Translated by S. Grayzel, "The Confessions of a Medieval Convert," *Historia Judaica* 17 (1955): 89–120.

[186] See, on this, Grayzel, *XIIIth Century*, Appendix B, pp. 341–43.

[187] Eisenstein, *Oṣar*, p. 86 and ed. Greenbaum, p. 12.

[188] In Browe, *Judenmission*, p. 76, n. 69.

[189] In E. Langlois, *Les Registres de Nicolas IV* (Paris, 1905) nos. 3573–75, p. 552; and cf. J. Vidal, *Bullaire de l'inquisition française* (Paris, 1913, no. 318).

[190] In Saige, *Languedoc*, pp. 238–39; and cf. Bat Sheva Albert on Jean Fournier in *The Case of Baruch* (Ramat Gan, 1974), p. 46.

[191] Thus ibn Verga in "Shmad 41" near the end (*Shebet Yehudah*, ed. Shohat, p. 114), tells of the Pope, Marco Florentine (sic), who suddenly ceased protecting the Jews, ordered a synagogue destroyed, and demanded the restitution of interest already collected, when the Jews went beyond canonical limits and asked to retain a synagogue standing alongside a church. The implication about the need to learn limits is self-evident.

[192] In Finkelstein, *JSG*, pp. 330–31, and trans., p. 338: ". . . in a matter disputed by the religions, even if a Jew (by believing it) should strengthen the convictions of a Christian heretic, he should not be plagued by the scourge of heresy (and be brought before the Inquisition) . . . Rather, he should be punished for this by the (secular) ruler. . . ." This last remark, primarily tactical, was probably intended to indicate more a distrust of the Inquisition than faith in the king.

[193] See J. Vidal, *Bullaire de l'inquisition française*, nos. 269–70, giving Gregory XI's 1372 reissue of Boniface's letter, *Exhibita Nobis* (June 13, 1299).

[194] Cited in J. H. Mundy, *Europe in the High Middle Ages* (New York, 1973), p. 323, citing *Notitia seculi* in *MGH Staatschriften* I, i, 154. Interestingly, Mundy refers here to a Jewish reference to the pope as "king of the Nations."

[195] Cited and trans. by David Ruderman, "A Jewish Apologetic Treatise from Sixteenth Century Bologna," *HUCA* 50 (1979): 265.

[196] In Joinville, *Histoire de Saint Louis*, ed. N. de Wailly (Paris, 1874), 31; noted in Grayzel, *XIIIth Century*, p. 26, n. 23.

[197] Grayzel, *XIIIth Century*, p. 280.

[198] Issued on Aug. 4, 1278; see J. Sbaralea *Bullarium Franciscanum* (Rome, 1759–1904) 3: 331, no. 50; for a discussion of forced preaching, see K. Stow, *Catholic Thought*,

p. 20, n. 59. It is important for perspective to compare *Vineam sorec* to *Sancta mater ecclesia* of Gregory XIII (1584); the latter *orders* attendance. But, then, by 1584, the papacy had abandoned its medieval Jewry policy and turned to one of near forced conversion; see *ibid.*

[199] For this text, see I. Loeb in *Revue des Études Juives* 1 (1880): 115 f.

[200] Caesar of Heisterbach's tale is translated by Jacob Marcus, *Jew in the Medieval World* (Phila., 1938), pp. 142–44; the bull *Cum de tam* was published by S. Grayzel in *JQR* 46 (1955): 61–63.

[201] The term was introduced by Innocent III as a motto indicating the restrictive side of canon Jewry law; see Grayzel, *XIIIth Century*, pp. 114–15; Stow, "Hatred," p. 106; and Langmuir, "Tanquam servi," pp. 50–51.

[202] See Jordan, *Louis IX*, pp. 156–57.

[203] Special note must be made of the Fourth Lateran Decrees (1215), which are usually portrayed as a hardening of the Church's position. However, a perusal of the literature cited in nn. 56 and 65 above, as well as of the pertinent passages in Gratian and the *Decretals*, reveals, on the contrary, the development over the centuries of a coherent and consistent legal doctrine into which the legislation of 1215 quite logically fits; see Stow, *Catholic Thought*, pp. 80–111 and Appendix II, part I.

[204] It would be amiss *not* to mention Grayzel's contention that by the later thirteenth century, the popes were stressing restriction out of proportion to their calls for protection and that by so doing they were not only undercutting the importance and effectiveness of *Sicut Iudaeis*, but indirectly encouraging extremism too; see *XIIIth Century*, pp. 81–82 and "Popes, Jews and Inquisition," *passim*. In contrast, and as argued here, I believe the Jews of the 13th Century correctly understood the papal stress on restriction and protection to be both equal and constant. The Jewish task was to insure that this equilibrium remained in place.

[205] See here, Friedberg, *De finium*, *passim*, and Jean Gaudemet in Lot and Fawtier, *Histoire des Institutions* 3: 273–79, for a discussion of the overall problem. With reference to the Jews, their *servi*, or *quasi-servi*, kings were always hesitant about sharing their powers; cf. the references above, esp. n. 141. The following point is pertinent here: while kings might concede that Jews should be punished for certain "spiritual" transgressions, still they insisted: "Cum non sint de fide seu lege catholica et si aliquo excesserint contra legem, (canonicam), sunt per nos puniendi," (James I of Aragon [20 June 1292], in Baer, *Die Juden* 1: 148, no. 1338).

תמצא לך [illegible] · [illegible] · כנגד ד׳ מלכיות שהיו עתידין לעמוד
על ישר׳ · [illegible] להם הקב״ה בניי [illegible] שלא יטעו אתכם אומות העולם [illegible]
עתיד לפרוע מהם בסוף · הה״ד פוקד עון אבות · פוקד עונו של נבוכד נצר
על בלשצר · על שלשים [illegible] [illegible] ועל רבעים
זו [illegible] [illegible] [illegible] · [illegible] זו אדום הרשעה [illegible] עשו [illegible]
[illegible] · ועושה חסד לאלפים · וכיון [illegible] [illegible] הקב״ה [illegible] [illegible]
[illegible] עד שיפרע [illegible] העולם · וכן בדברי קבלה [illegible] [illegible]
[illegible] [illegible] שוכן בציון · כת׳ [illegible] [illegible] [illegible] [illegible] עמד
[illegible] וגו׳ · [illegible] [illegible] [illegible] הקב״ה [illegible] [illegible] [illegible]
[illegible] [illegible] לך [illegible] י״י אלהיך · [illegible] כל ישר׳ [illegible] [illegible] י״י אלהיכם [illegible]
[illegible] [illegible] על בניי [illegible] [illegible] להם [illegible] [illegible] י״י
אלהיך [illegible] [illegible] [illegible] לכם [illegible] י״י אלהיכם להחזיר את כולכם
[illegible] [illegible] [illegible] [illegible] [illegible] [illegible] וגו׳ עד כאן · [illegible]
[illegible] [illegible] [illegible] · [illegible] [illegible] יעקב כי [illegible] [illegible] סליק
[illegible] בשנת ארבעת אלפים ושבע מאות וששים ושבע לבריאת
עולם גזרה מלכות הרשעה שמד על ישר׳ [illegible] [illegible] [illegible]
[illegible] [illegible] [illegible] [illegible] סוד [illegible] [illegible] [illegible]
כל היהודים [illegible] [illegible] · [illegible] [illegible] [illegible] [illegible] [illegible]
[illegible] [illegible] [illegible] [illegible] [illegible] [illegible] [illegible] [illegible] [illegible]
[illegible] [illegible] [illegible] [illegible] [illegible] [illegible] · [illegible] [illegible] [illegible]
[illegible] [illegible] ישר׳ כי [illegible] [illegible] [illegible] [illegible] בכל [illegible] [illegible] [illegible]
[illegible] [illegible] [illegible] [illegible] · [illegible] [illegible] [illegible] [illegible] [illegible]
[illegible] [illegible] [illegible] · [illegible] [illegible] [illegible] [illegible] [illegible] [illegible]
[illegible] [illegible] [illegible] [illegible] [illegible] [illegible] [illegible] [illegible]

[illegible] עם שרי [illegible] לעם
יהוד [illegible] שלשים [illegible] ושובו [illegible] כי [illegible] יותר [illegible]
ויום [illegible] על פי [illegible] לכם [illegible]
על זה [illegible] ויצאו [illegible] לפני [illegible]
השם ויחזק לבם [illegible] בן [illegible] ויבא [illegible]
לא [illegible] לך בדבר זה לכפר [illegible] עשה [illegible]
[illegible] להרג על קדושות השם [illegible] הגדול [illegible]
חסידי עליון [illegible] כמים [illegible] את ישר׳ להרג [illegible]
[illegible] ובעת ההיא [illegible] ביד [illegible]
[illegible] מלכו [illegible] שם שרים על
[illegible] כי היה [illegible] וטוב לנו מות
מחיים [illegible] על [illegible] על נפשו הבן ולא הבן
[illegible] השם הנכבד [illegible] היה כן [illegible]
[illegible] הרשעים [illegible] כי לא [illegible] להם
[illegible] ישר׳ [illegible]
[illegible] עליו [illegible]
[illegible]
[illegible] סוסיהם [illegible] ויקם [illegible]
[illegible] לכם [illegible] על ישר׳ [illegible]
[illegible] כי [illegible] על פי [illegible]
[illegible] ויבא
[illegible] על ישר׳ [illegible]
[illegible]
[illegible] על [illegible] בן

בקשרי ירבעתיו ודקור כפו· ויאמר היהודי שאול מן לירים ריקשוני
יהשר חיו לפניך ויגיד לך שכל זה שעשה רעה ליהודים וזה ידע להם
ויאמר הרשע ידעתי כי השכיל שדקר ידי ביחידות החרב כי ידין ג
עתה שעה להורגך שהיהודים ירחם עליך· והעשה כאלו שיראת ויש
ומלאך יהל היופיפיור וכל יהשר יאמר עשה רק יהוד הכבוך יקדר
[illegible] לבלתי תשחוק בי· וידעתי שששון ככם הנה יהל ויאמר שהתפילה
[illegible] לין יכולתי לבטלה כי יום על פי ריגש הגים· ועתה לך לשם ועשי
[illegible] יהל ירחוו עליכם מן הטהרים· ושם הרשע ר׳ יעקב בר יהודה
ויושט הנה וירכב עמו יהודה ויפתח ויוסף ויהודה· ושם יהודה
במרכבן ביד הערל· ויסע הוא והושט ושלשת עמו וירכב עבריו
ושמם עשר סוסין ויבאו עד רוחין בעזרת השם שישו ברוך
וישמח לשני היופיפיור ולא כרע ולא השתחוה לו· כי דרך הגים להשתחו
ויאל במנין והוד ויאמר לו מי יתמם ויעביהו יהודי יהב וירדין רחוקה
ביותי יהליך יהוב והשתי וכבי וביותי לבקש עבו יתן לי מקום לדבר
יותך כתב וכמו כי דבר סתר ישלי יהליך· ויקם מעל כסאו וישב כל
העם ויכבו שמחים בחדל יחוד· ויאמר לו יעקב יהודי יום הייתי יכול
לעלות לשרים לספר ריותני ויור יעבר עלי יהכל לא הימותי עמה והלתי
הענר מושל להעלה ויתן בקריצת הגים כי ריגש היותות יתשר ושליט
עליהם על כן ביותי להעין יהליך על רעתי מן היהודים היושבים עמות
במחשבות רשותך כי קוה עליהם זכרי מלשל כל רשותך והרג והחם
הרבה ולמסור חיקיעתם· ועתה יום טוב בעיניך ותמסור להשפיטם
ושלם הוחזק ושלחך והרם ידך עליהם שלא יהיה בני ישראל להרוג
ישר׳ בשום ענין ולא להזיקו ולא לענותו והמכשו ולא להכריחו והשיבו
לשמות· והנה בידי היותים ליט הימים ותעבטו והיהודים ליהודי יבש

כי היה יושב ויתן זה על יד משרתך להכין יו' לבית גנזיו ושבעה ויקרים זהב
ושקל להמון שהביאה שילך כשליחותך ויתן לו טבעת עשר סוסים למרכבתו
ומיתנים שקלי כסף להוצאות הדרך ויאסור בידו כתב חותמו כל קהילות ישר'
שיכבדוהו ויהי יהיה עמך עד שישוב המלך לשלום ויאמר ההושפיטור ותנו
לו זמן חמשה עשר יום ויועצו עם הגמוני ושרי הכמרים ויושיבך דבר ויתנו לו
ויושיבך עד הזמן עם היהודים יודי פני ויען יוחנן ר' יעקב לחיים ולשלום
וישלח בעבור ראשי העיר והם ר' משה המשיין ור' אברהם ור' שבתאי הכהני
העיר ויפקד בידם זה הדיש ויצו עליהם שיכבדוהו ויאמר ולך הטרב עם הקצינים
ויכינו לו בית ולאנשיו ולכבוד ולסוסיו ועבדיו כי היה בידו כל טוב ולא רצה ליהנות
משל יהודים ויגד ליהודים דברי הגזירה וכל יושר לו וידע להם מיד ויתפללו יו'
שיהיה לב ההושפיטור שלם עמהם ויהי יום בין השמש ויבוא ר' יעקב ושלושת
הרבנים עמו לפני ההושפיטור וישאלו לקראתו ויקריבו לו לשלום ויען הרבי יוחנן
ממשלחתך ויגש לו החותם כל יושר שיל וישלח הגמוני והחתום בידו וילך לרבים
הדיש המכבד נשיא בעיר רומי ויכבדו עד שוב ההגמון מכל הקהילות [illegible]
[illegible] שלו עבר עליהם וביטל הגזרה הגזירה על ידו של יוחנן חסיד וכחו לו
[illegible] לטובה [illegible] יהודית ותקוה ישה כל יהודת עולם ויקח
[illegible] ההושפיטור ושלחהו מיריםכבוד ויאמר לו יום [illegible] לשום דבר
[illegible] שלח לי שלומך ואל תבוא עמוך יומר כי יעשה כל רצונך וישב יו' [illegible]
[illegible] ויהי שנים עשר שנה ולקץ הימים שלח [illegible] תחת [illegible]
[illegible] יוחנן הקיבנן [illegible] שלושים יהודים [illegible]
[illegible] ויקם וילך [illegible] ויעמוד עמו שלשה חדשים ויקבל
[illegible] עם שני [illegible] וילך שנה לבית עליון [illegible]
[illegible] לחזון [illegible] ישב על [illegible] ידיו על פניו [illegible]
[illegible] וישוחו [illegible] ויקברוהו שם [illegible]

איזורים ותמה נפשו ביסורי הגויים ״ סליק״

x x מעשה ברבי מאיר ״ שהיה עולה לירושלים אחת לשלש

שנים ומתארח אצל טבח אחד ואותו הטבח היתה אשתו צדקת ומכבדתו

ביותר והיה [illegible] מרבה במעשים כשרים ובנה לו בית וחדר [illegible] שם כסא

שולחן ומנורה והולך לדרכו. לקץ עשר שנים מתה אשת אותו הטבח ונשא אחרת.

ויבא ר׳ מאיר כמנהגו ונשק על פתח [illegible] ואמרה לו [illegible] לשלום

[illegible] לו [illegible] אשת [illegible] [illegible] אשת [illegible]

[illegible] לו [illegible] ואשת [illegible] ירד מן החמור ובכה [illegible] לו ר׳ [illegible]

[illegible] בכבודך [illegible] [illegible] בבית [illegible] [illegible] [illegible]

[illegible] ר׳ מאיר [illegible] בבית [illegible] [illegible] [illegible]

[illegible] [illegible] [illegible] [illegible] [illegible]

[illegible] [illegible] [illegible] [illegible] [illegible]

[illegible] [illegible] [illegible] [illegible] ר׳ [illegible]

[illegible] [illegible] [illegible] [illegible] [illegible] בבית [illegible]

[illegible] על [illegible] [illegible] [illegible] [illegible]

[illegible] [illegible] [illegible] [illegible] ביום

השלישי [illegible] [illegible] [illegible] [illegible]

[illegible] [illegible] [illegible] [illegible] [illegible]

[illegible] ר׳ מאיר [illegible] [illegible] [illegible]

[illegible] [illegible] [illegible] [illegible]

[illegible] [illegible] [illegible] [illegible]

[illegible] [illegible] [illegible] [illegible]

[illegible] [illegible] [illegible] [illegible]

[illegible] [illegible] [illegible] [illegible]

Bibliography

Manuscripts

Oxford, Ms. Oxford-Bodleian 847 (Microfilm Institute of the Hebrew University and National Library, no. 21608).
Parma, Biblioteca Palatina, ms. de Rossi 563.
Parma, Biblioteca Palatina, ms. 2749.

Sources

Alexander of Hales. *Summa Theologica*. 4 vols. Quaracchi, 1924–28.
Anonymous. "ᶜEdut ᵓAdonai Neᵓemana," in J. Rosenthal ed. *Meḥqarim u-Meqorot*, 2 vols. Jerusalem, 1967.
Augustinus, Aurelius. "Adversus Iudaeos," in J. P. Migne, *Patrologia Latina*, vol. 42. Paris, 1844–1905.
Baldus de Ubaldis. *Consilia*. 1575.
Baronius, Caesar. *Annales Ecclesiastici*, ed. J. D. Mansi. Lucca, 1744.
Beinart, Haim. *Kitve Zekhuyot Klalliyot shel Yehudei Eiropah*. Jerusalem, 1972.
Bouquet, Martin. *Recueil des Historiens des Gaules et de la France*, vol. 20. Paris, 1840.
______. *Receuil des Historiens des Croisades, Historiens Occidentaux*. Paris, 1841–1879.
Bullarium Diplomatum et Privilegiorum Taurensis Editio. Turin, 1857–72.
The Catechism of the Council of Trent, trans. J. Donovan. New York, 1929.
Corpus Iuris Canonici, ed. E. Friedberg. 2 vols. Leipzig, 1879–81.
Corpus Iuris Civilis, ed. Kreuger-Mommsen. 3 vols. Berlin, 1905, 1906, 1928.
Carmoly, A. "Toldoth," *Oṣar Neḥmad* 3 (1860): 105–112.
Denifle, Heinrich. "Quellen zur Disputation Pablos Christiani mit Mose Nachmani zu Barcelona, 1263," *Historisches Jahrbuch des Goerres Gesellschaft* 8 (1887): 225–44.
Duemmler, E., ed. *Agobardi Lugdunensis Archiepiscopi Epistolae, Monumenta Germaniae Historica Epistolae*, 3 vols. Berlin, 1829. Epistolae Karolini Aevi III.
Eisenstein, J. B. *Oṣar Wikuḥim*. New York, 1929.
Eshtori ha-Parḥi. *Kaftor va-Peraḥ*. Jerusalem, 1899.

Grayzel, Solomon. "The Confessions of a Medieval Convert," *Historia Judaica* 17 (1955): 89–120.

Haberman, A. M. *Sefer Gezerot Ṣarfat Ve-ʾAshkenaz.* Jerusalem, 1971.

Ha-Cohen, Yosef. *ʿEmeq ha-Bakha*, ed. M. Letteris. Cracow, 1895.

Harkavy, Abraham. "A Letter to R. David, Maimonides' Grandson," *Ha-Kedem* 3 (1912): 111–14.

Hasdai, Crescas. *Bitul ʿIqarei Dat Ha-Noṣrim*, ed. E. Deinard. Kearny, N.J., 1904.

Helgaud de Fleury. *Vie de Robert le Pieux*, ed. and trans. R. H. Bautier and G. Labory, Paris, 1965.

Jaffe, Philip. *Monumenta Gregoriana.* Berlin, 1865.

Jellinek, Ad. *Bet-Hamidrash.* Jerusalem, 1938. 6 parts.

Joinville. *Histoire de Saint Louis*, ed. N. de Wailly, Paris, 1874.

Josef b. Natan Official. *Sefer Yosef Ha-Meqane*, ed. J. Rosenthal. Jerusalem, 1970.

Kitve Ha-Rambam, ed. H. D. Chavel. 2 vols. Jerusalem, 1963.

de Lauriere, E. J. *Ordonnances des rois de la troisième race.* 22 vols. Paris, 1723–1849.

Langlois, E. *Les Registres de Nicolas IV.* Paris, 1905.

Loewenfeld, Samuel. *Epistolae Pontificum Romanorum ineditae.* Leipzig, 1885.

Luther, Martin. *Against the Sabbatarians. Luther's Works*, vol. 47, ed. and trans. M. Bertram. Philadelphia, 1971.

Luzzato, S. D. *Bet Ha-Oṣar.* Lvov, 1881.

Mansi, J. D. *Sacrorum Conciliorum Collectio*, 59 vols. Venice, 1759–98. (reprint, Graz, 1960–61).

Martene, E. and Durand, U. *Thesaurus novus anecdotorum.* Paris, 1717.

Migne, J. P. *Patrologia, Cursus Completus. Series Latina.* Paris, 1844–1905. *Series Graeca.* Paris, 1856.

Müller, J. *Teshuvot Hakhme Ṣarfat Ve-Lotair.* Vienna, 1881.

Penaforte, Raymond. *Summa de Poenitentia et Matrimonio.* Rome, 1603.

Pertz, G. H., ed. *Monumenta Germaniae Historica. Scriptores XI.* Hanover, 1854 (reprint, Stuttgart, 1968).

Profiat Duran. *Sefer Klimat ha-Goyim.* ed. N. Posnanski. *Ha-Ṣofeh Me-ʾereṣ Hagar* 3 (1913) and 4 (1914).

Ramackers, Johannes. *Papsturkunden in Frankreich.* Berlin, 1932–33.

Raymundus Martinus. *Pugio Fidei*, ed. Johannes Carpzov. Leipzig, 1687.

Rymer, Thomas. *Foedera.* vol. I (London, 1816).

Sbaralea, J. *Bullarium Franciscanum.* Rome, 1759–1904.

Seder Eliyahu Zuta, ed. S. Simonsohn and M. Benayahu. 3 vols. Jerusalem and Tel Aviv, 1977 and 1983.

Sefer Yossipon, ed. D. Flusser, 2 vols. Jerusalem, 1978–79.

Shelomo ibn Verga. *Shebet Yehudah*, ed. A. Shohat. Jerusalem, 1956.

Stern, Moritz. *Urkundliche Beitraege ueber die Stellung der Paepste zu den Juden.* Kiel, 1893; and Westmead: Gregg (reprint), 1970.

Stubbs, William. *Select Charters and Other Illustrations of English Constitutional History from the Earliest Times to the Reign of Edward The First.* Oxford, 1962.

de Susannis, Marquardus. *De Iudaeis et Aliis Infidelibus.* Venice, 1558.

Talmage, Frank, ed. *The Polemical Writings of Profiat Duran* [in Hebrew]. Jerusalem, 1981.

Vidal, J. M. *Bullaire de l'inquisition française au XIVe siècle.* Paris, 1913.

"Vikuaḥ R. Ya'acov Mivinișya," ed. J. Kabak, *Ginze Nistarot,* Bamberg, 1868.

Vikuaḥ Rabbi Yeḥiel Mi-Paris, ed. Shemuel Greenbaum. Thorn, 1873.

Wagenseil, J. C., ed. *Tela Ignea Satanae.* Frankfurt a.M., 1861.

Yosef Albo. *Sefer Ha-'Ikkarim/Book of Principles,* ed. I. Husik. Philadelphia, 1946.

Works

Agus, I. A. "Control of Roads by Jews in Pre-Crusade Europe," *Jewish Quarterly Review* 48 (1957): 93–98.

Albert, B. S. *The Case of Baruch* [in Hebrew]. Ramat Gan, 1974.

Aronius, Julius. *Regesten zur Geschichte der Juden in Frankischen und Deutschen Reiche bis zum Jahre 1273.* Berlin, 1902.

Baer, Yitzhak. "The Historical Background of the Raya Mehamna" [in Hebrew], *Zion* 5 (1940): 1–44.

Baer, Yitzhak. *A History of the Jews in Christian Spain.* 2 vols. Philadelphia, 1966.

Baldwin, J. W. *Masters, Princes and Merchants,* 2 vols. Princeton, 1970.

Barber, Malcolm. "The World Picture of Philip the Fair," *Journal of Medieval History* 8 (1982): 13–27.

Baron, S. W. "Plenitude of Apostolic Powers and Medieval Jewish Serfdom," *Ancient and Medieval Jewish History.* New Brunswick, N.J., 1972, pp. 284–307.

Baron, S. W. *A Social and Religious History of the Jews,* 17 vols. Philadelphia, 1952–80.

Becker, Marvin. *Medieval Italy: Constraints and Creativity.* Bloomington, Indiana, 1981.

Ben Sasson, H. H. "La-Megamah ha-Kronografiah ha-Yehudit shel Yeme ha-Beinayim," *Ha-Historyon Ve-ʾAskolot ha-Historia.* Jerusalem, 1963, pp. 29–49.

Benton, J. F., ed. *Self and Society in Medieval France.* New York, 1970.

Benz, Ernst. *Ecclesia Spiritualis.* Stuttgart, 1934.

Berger, David. "The Attitude of St. Bernard of Clairvaux Toward the Jews," *Proceedings of the American Academy for Jewish Research* 40 (1972): 89–108.

______. *The Jewish Christian Debate in the High Middle Ages.* Philadelphia, 1979.

Blumenkranz, Bernhard. *Les auteurs Chrétiens Latins du Moyen Age sur les Juifs et le Judaïsme*. Paris, 1963.

______. "Deux compilations Canoniques de Florus de Lyon et l'action antijuive d'Agobard," *Revue Historique de Droit Français et Etranger* 33 (1955): 227–54, 560–62.

______. *Die Judenpredigt Augustins*. Basle, 1946.

______. *Juifs et Chrétiens dans le Monde Occidental*. Paris, 1960.

Bonenfant, Paul. "Du Duché de basse Lotharingie au Duché de Brabant," *Revue Belge de Philologie et d'Histoire* 46 (1968): 1129–65.

Bonfil, Robert. "The Nature of Judaism in Raymundus Martini's Pugio Fidei" [in Hebrew], *Tarbiz* 40 (1971): 360–75.

Brentano, Robert. *Rome Before Avignon*. New York, 1974.

Browe, Petrus. *Die Judenmission im Mittelalter und die Paepste*. Rome, 1942.

Carlyle, A. J. *A History of Medieval Political Theory in the West*, 6 vols. New York, 1936.

Caro, Georg. *Sozial und Wirtschaftsgeschichte der Juden im Mittelalter und der Neuzeit*. Leipzig, 1908–20.

Catalano, G. *Impero, Regno e Sacerdozio nel Pensiero di Uguccio da Pisa*. Milano, 1959.

Chazan, Robert. "Anti-Usury Efforts in Thirteenth Century Narbonne and the Jewish Response," *Proceedings of the American Academy for Jewish Research*, 41–42 (1973–74): 45–67.

______. "Confrontation in the Synagogue of Narbonne: A Christian Sermon and a Jewish Reply," *Harvard Theological Review* 67 (1974): 437–57.

______. "1007–1012, Initial Crisis for Northern European Jewry," *Proceedings of the American Academy for Jewish Research* 39 (1972): 101–18.

______. "A Jewish Plaint to Saint Louis," *Hebrew Union College Annual* 45 (1974): 287–305.

______. *Medieval Jewry in Northern France*. Baltimore, 1973.

Chodorow, Stanley. *Christian Political Theory and Church Politics in the Mid-Twelfth Century*. Berkeley, 1972.

Cohen, Jeremy. *The Friars and the Jews*. Ithaca, 1982.

Colorni, Vittore. *Legge Ebraica e Leggi Locali*. Milan, 1945.

Congar, Yves. *L'Ecclésiologie du Hâut Moyen Age*. Paris, 1968.

Cowdrey, H. E. J. "Pope Gregory VII and The Anglo-Norman Church and Kingdom," *Studi Gregoriani* 9 (1972): 83–96.

Delisle, Leopold. "Des Revenus Publics en Normandie au Douzieme Siècle," *Bibliothèque de l'Ecole des Chartres* 10 (1848–49): 178–210.

Dienstag, J. I. "St. Thomas Aquinas in Maimonidian Scholarship," *Studies in Maimonides and St. Thomas Aquinas*. New York, 1975. pp. 192–206.

Duby, Georges. *L'An Mil*. Paris, 1974 (reprint of 1967).

Duchesne, P. *The Beginnings of the Temporal Authority of the Popes*. trans. A. M. Matthew. New York, 1972 (reprint of 1908).

Emery, R. W. *The Jews of Perpignan*. New York, 1959.

Encyclopaedia Judaica. Jerusalem, 1971.

Evans, Austin and Wakefield, Walter. *Heresies of the High Middle Ages*. New York, 1969.

Finkelstein, Louis. *Jewish Self Government in the Middle Ages*. New York, 1964. (reprint of 1924).

Foreville, Raymonde. "The Synods of the Province of Rouen in the Eleventh and Twelfth Centuries," *Essays Presented to C. R. Cheney*, ed., C. N. L. Brooke, et al., Cambridge, 1976.

Fournial, Etienne. *Histoire Monétaire de l'Occident Médiéval*. Paris, 1970.

Friedberg, Emil. *De Finium inter Ecclesiam et Civitatem Regundorum Judicio*. Leipzig, 1965 (reprint of 1861).

Funkenstein, Amos. "Changes in the Patterns of Anti-Jewish Polemics in the 12th Century" [in Hebrew], *Zion* 33 (1968): 137–42.

Gaster, Moses. *The Maᶜaseh Book*. Philadelphia, 1934.

Gay, Jules. *Les Papes du XIᵉ Siècle*. New York, 1972 (reprint).

Genicot, Leopold. *Etudes sur les Principautés Lotharingiennes*. Louvain, 1965.

Golb, Norman. *History and Culture of the Jews of Rouen in the Middle Ages* [in Hebrew]. Tel Aviv, 1976.

______. "New Light on the Persecution of French Jews at the Time of the First Crusade," *Proceedings of the American Academy for Jewish Research* 34 (1966): 1–64.

Graetz, Heinrich. *Geschichte der Juden*. 11 vols. Leipzig, 1853–76.

Grayzel, Solomon. *The Church and the Jews in the XIIIth Century*. Philadelphia, 1933.

______. "Jewish References in a Thirteenth Century Formulary," *Jewish Quarterly Review* 46 (1955): 61–63.

______. "The Papal Bull 'Sicut Iudaeis.'" *Studies and Essays in Honor of Abraham A. Neuman*. Leiden, 1962: pp. 243–80.

______. "Pope Alexander III and the Jews." *Salo W. Baron Jubilee Volume*. Jerusalem, 1975, pp. 561–62.

______. "Popes, Jews and Inquisition - from '*Sicut*' to '*Turbato*.'" *Essays on the Occasion of the Seventieth Anniversary of the Dropsie University*. Philadelphia, 1979. pp. 151–88.

Guilhiermoz, P. "Note sur les poids du moyen age," *Bibliothèque de l'Ecole des Chartres* 67 (1906): 200.

Hauck, Albert. *Real Encyklopaedie für Protestantische Theologie und Kirche*. Graz, 1971 (reprint).

Heers, Jacques. *Le Clan Familial au Moyen Age*. Paris, 1974.

Hendrix, Scott. "In Quest of the *Vera Ecclesia*: The Crises of Late Medieval Ecclesiology," *Viator* 7 (1976): 347–78.

Herlihy, David. "The Agrarian Revolution in France and Italy: 801–1150," *The Social History of Italy and Western Europe 700–1500*. London, 1978.

Hollister, C. W. and Baldwin, J. W. "The Rise of Administrative Kingship: Henry I and Philip Augustus," *American Historical Review*, 83 (1978): 867–905.

Holt, J. C. *Magna Carta*. Cambridge, 1965.

Holtzmann, Walter. "Zur paepstlichen Gesetzgebung ueber die Juden im 12ten Jahrhundert." *Festschrift Guido Kisch*. Stuttgart, 1955. pp. 217–35.

Jackson, Gabriel. *The Making of Medieval Spain*. New York, 1972.

Jordan, Wm. C. *Louis IX and the Challenge of the Crusade: A Study in Rulership*. Princeton, 1979.

Kantorowicz, E. H. *The King's Two Bodies*. Princeton, 1957.

———. "Kingship and Scientific Jurisprudence." *Twelfth Century Europe and the Foundations of Modern Society*. Ed. M. Clagett et al., Madison, 1961.

Katz, Jacob. *Exclusiveness and Tolerance*. New York, 1962.

Kedar, B. Z. "Canon Law and the Burning of the Talmud," *Bulletin of Medieval Canon Law* 9 (1979): 79–82.

Kisch, Guido. *The Jews in Medieval Germany*. 2nd ed. New York, 1970.

Kneiwasser, Manfred. "Bischof Agobard von Lyon und die Juden in einer Sakral Verfassten Einheits Gesellschaft," *Kairos* 19 (1979): 203–27.

Krauss, Samuel. "Apiphior, Nom Hébreu du Pape," *Revue des Etudes Juives* 34–35 (1897): 218–38.

Kriegel, Maurice. "Mobilisation Politique et Modernisation Organique," *Archives de Sciences Sociales* 46 (1978): 5–20.

———. "Prémarranisme et inquisition dans la Provence des XIIIe et XIVe siècles," *Provence Historique* 29 (1978): 313–23.

Kuttner Stephan. "Universal Pope or Servant of God's Servants: The Canonists, Papal Titles and Innocent III," *Revue de Droit Canonique* 32 (1981): 109–49.

Ladner, Gerhard. "The Concepts of '*Ecclesia*' and '*Christianitas*'. Their relation to the Idea of Papal '*plenitudo potestatis*' from Gregory VII to Boniface VIII," *Sacerdozio e Regno da Gregorio VII a Bonifacio VIII*. Rome, 1954.

———. *The Idea of Reform*. Cambridge, Mass., 1959.

de Lagarde, Georges. *La naissance de l'esprit laïque au déclin du moyen âge*, 5 vols., 3rd ed. Paris, 1956.

Langmuir, Gavin. "The Jews and the Archives of Angevin England," *Traditio* 19 (1963): 183–244.

———. "'Judei Nostri' and the Beginnings of Capetian Legislation," *Traditio* 16 (1963): 203–69.

———. "From Ambrose of Milan to Emicho of Leiningen: The Transformation of Hostility Against Jews in Northern Christendom," *Gli Ebrei nell'Alto Medioevo*, Settimane di Studio 26. Spoleto, 1980. pp. 313–68.

———. "Review of B. Bachrach, Early Medieval Jewish Policy," *Speculum* 54 (1979): 104.

———. "Tanquam Servi: The Change in Jewish Status in French Law About 1200," *Les Juifs dans l'Histoire de France*, ed. M. Yardeni. Leiden, 1980, pp. 24–54.

Le Bras, Gabriel. *Institutions Ecclésiastiques de la chrétienté médiévale*. Paris, 1964.

Lemarignier, J. F. *Le Gouvernment Royal aux Premiers Temps Capétiens (987–1108)*. Paris, 1965.

———. "Les Institutions Ecclésiastiques en France de la fin du Xe siècle," eds. F. Lot et R. Fawtier, *Histoire des Institutions Françaises au Moyen Age.* Paris, 1962.

Levi, Israel. "Les Juifs de France du milieu du IXe siècle aux croisades," *Revue des Etudes Juives* 52 (1906): 161–68.

Liebeschutz, Hans. "The Crusading Movement and Its Bearing on Christian Attitudes Towards Jewry," *Journal of Jewish Studies* 10 (1959): 97–111.

Llorca, Bernardino. "Derechos de la Santa Sede sobre España. El pensamiento de Gregorio VII," *Sacerdozio e Regno.* Rome, 1954. Pp. 79–106.

Loeb, Isidore. "Bulles inédites des papes," *Revue des Etudes Juives* 1 (1880): 116–17.

Lunt, W. E. *Papal Revenues in the Middle Ages.* New York, 1934.

Maccarone, Michele. "'Potestas directa' e 'Potestas indirecta' nei teologi del XII e XIII secolo," *Sacerdozio e Regno.* Rome, 1954.

Mann, Jacob. *Texts and Studies.* New York, 1972 (reprint).

Marcus, Jacob. *The Jew in the Medieval World.* Philadelphia, 1938. (reprint, New York, 1965).

Menache, Sophia. "Vers une conscience nationale: mythe et symbolisme au début de la guerre de Cent Ans," *Le Moyen Age* 89 (1983): 85–97.

Merchavia, Ch. M. *The Church versus Talmudic and Midrashic Literature.* Jerusalem, 1970.

Morrison, K. F. *The Two Kingdoms, Ecclesiology in Carolingian Political Thought.* Princeton, 1964.

———. *Tradition and Authority in the Western Church, 300–1140.* Princeton, 1969.

Mundy, J. H. *Europe in the High Middle Ages.* New York, 1973.

Nahon, Gerard. "Le Crédit et les Juifs dans la France du XIIIe siècle," *Annales* 24 (1969): 1137–38.

Pakter, Walter. *De His Qui Foris Sunt: The Teachings of the Medieval Canon and Civil Lawyers Concerning the Jews.* Dissertation. Johns Hopkins University. Baltimore, 1974.

Parkes, James. *The Conflict of the Church and the Synagogue.* Philadelphia, 1961 (reprint).

Pfister, Charles. *Etudes sur le règne de Robert le Pieux (996–1031).* Paris, 1885.

Pilati, Giovanni. *Chiesa e Stato nei primi quindici secoli.* Rome, 1961.

Post, Gaines. "Two Notes on Nationalism in the Middle Ages," *Traditio* 9 (1953): 281–320.

Rembaum, Joel. "The Talmud and the Popes: Reflections on the Talmud Trials of the 1240s," *Viator* 13 (1982): 203–23.

de Roover, Raymond. *Money, Banking and Credit in Mediaeval Bruges.* Cambridge, Mass., 1948.

Roth, Cecil. *A History of the Jews in England.* Oxford, 1949.

Ruderman, David. "A Jewish Apologetic Treatise from Sixteenth Century Bologna," *Hebrew Union College Annual* 50 (1979): 253–76.

Russell, Frederick. *The Just War in the Middle Ages.* Cambridge, 1978.

Saige, Gustave. *Les Juifs du Languedoc*. Paris, 1881.

Saperstein, Marc. *Decoding the Rabbis*. Cambridge, Mass., 1980.

Scheid, E. "Catalogue des Documents du Trésor des Chartres," *Revue des Etudes Juives* 2 (1881): 31.

Schiffmann, Sara. "Die deutschen Bischöfe und die Juden zur Zeit des ersten Kreuzzuges," *Zeitschrift für die Geschichte der Juden in Deutschland* 3 (1931): 233–50.

______. "Heinrichs IV Verhalten zu den Juden zur Zeit des ersten Kreuzzuges," *Zeitschrift für die Geschichte der Juden in Deutschland* 3 (1931): 39–58.

Schmidt, Tillman. *Alexander II und die Römische Reform Gruppe Seiner Zeit*. Stuttgart, 1977.

Schwarzfuchs, S. "Jacob bar Yekoutièl chez le Pape," *Evidences* 6 (1954): 36–37.

Segre, Renata. "Bernardino da Feltre, i Monti di pietà e i banchi ebraici," *Rivista Storica Italiana* 90 (1978): 818–33.

Shatzmiller, Joseph. "Did Nicholas Donin Promulgate the Blood Libel" [in Hebrew], *Studies in the History of the Jewish People and the Land of Israel* 4 (1978): 181–82.

______. "L'inquisition et les juifs de Provence au XIIe siècle," *Provence Historique* 23 (1973): 327–38.

Simonsohn, Shlomo. "Prolegomena to a History of the Relations between the Papacy and the Jews" [in Hebrew], *I. F. Baer Memorial Volume. Zion* 44 (1979): 66–93.

Singer, S. A. "The Expulsion of the Jews from England in 1290," *Jewish Quarterly Review* 55 (1964): 117–35.

Speigel, G. M. "'Defence of the Realm': Evolution of a Capetian Propaganda Slogan," *Journal of Medieval History* 3 (1977): 115–33.

Stein, Siegfried. *Jewish Christian Disputations in Thirteenth Century Narbonne*. London, 1969.

Stengers, Jean. *Les Juifs dans les Pays Bas au Moyen Age*. Brussels, 1950.

Stickler, A. M. "Concerning the Political Theories of the Medieval Canonists," *Traditio* 7 (1951): 450–63.

Stow, K. R. *Catholic Thought and Papal Jewry Policy*. New York, 1977.

______. "The Church and the Jews, From St. Paul to Paul IV," *Bibliographical Essays in Medieval Jewish Studies*. New York, 1976. pp. 107–65.

______. "Gishat ha-Yehudim la-ᵓApifiorut ve-ha-Doqtrinah ha-ᵓApifiorit shel Hagannat ha-Yehudim ba-Shanim 1063–1147" [in Hebrew], *Studies in the History of the Jewish People and the Land of Israel* 5 (1980): 75–90.

______. "Hatred of the Jews, or Love of the Church: Papal Policy Toward the Jews" [in Hebrew], *Antisemitism Through the Ages*, ed. S. Almog. Jerusalem, 1980. pp. 91–111.

______. "Jacob b. Elie and Jewish Settlement in Venice in the Thirteenth Century." Italia 4 (1985).

______. "Papal and Royal Attitudes Toward Jewish Lending in the Thirteenth Century," *AJS Review* 6 (1981): 161–84.

Strayer, Joseph. "France: The Holy Land, The Chosen People and the Most Christian King," *Medieval Statecraft and the Perspectives of History*. Princeton, 1971.

______. "The Laicization of French and English Society in the XIIIth Century," *Speculum* 15 (1940): 76–86.

Synan, Edward. *The Popes and the Jews in the Middle Ages*. New York, 1965.

Tykocinski, H. "Die Verfolgung der Juden in Mainz im Jahre 1012." *Festschrift M. Philippsons*, Leipzig, 1916, pp. 1–5.

Ullmann, Walter. *The Carolingian Renaissance and the Idea of Kingship*. London, 1969.

______. "Public Welfare and Social Legislation in the Early Medieval Councils," *Studies in Church History* 7 (1971): 23.

______. *A Short History of the Papacy in the Middle Ages*. London, 1977.

Vauchez, Andre. *La spiritualité du Moyen Age occidental VIIIe–XIIe siècles*. Paris, 1975.

Vogelstein, Hermann and Rieger, Paul. *Geschichte der Juden in Rom*. 2 vols. Berlin, 1895.

Watt, J. A. "The Term '*Plenitudo Potestatis*' in Hostiensis," *Proceedings of the Second International Congress of Medieval Canon Law*, ed. S. Kuttner. Vatican City, 1965.

Wilkens, R. L. and Meeks, W. A. *Jews and Christians in Antioch in the First Four Centuries of the Common Era*. Missoula, 1978.

Wilks, Michael. *The Problem of Sovereignty in the Later Middle Ages*. Cambridge, 1963.

Yerushalmi, Y. H. "The Inquisition and the Jews of France in the Time of Bernard Gui," *Harvard Theological Review* 63 (1970): 317–76.

______. *The Lisbon Massacre of 1506 and the Royal Image in the Shebet Yehudah*. Cincinnati, 1976.

Zema, D. B. "The Houses of Tuscany and of Pierleone in the Crisis of Rome in the Eleventh Century," *Traditio* 2 (1944): 155–75.

INDEX